GUIDE TO

ROCK

EAMONN FORDE

© Haynes Publishing 2020
Published July 2020

All rights reserved. No part of this publication
may be reproduced, stored in a retrieval system
or transmitted in any form or by any means, electronic,
mechanical, photocopying, recording or otherwise,
without the prior permission from Haynes Publishing.

A CIP Catalogue record for this book
is available from the British Library.

ISBN: 978 1 78521 583 4

Library of Congress control no. 2019953175

Published by J H Haynes & Co Ltd,
Sparkford, Yeovil, Somerset BA22 7JJ, UK
Tel: 01963 440635. Int. tel: +44 1963 440635
Website: www.haynes.com

Printed in Malaysia.

Bluffer's Guide®, Bluffer's® and Bluff Your Way®
are registered trademarks.

Series Editor: David Allsop.

CONTENTS

'Until I realised that rock music was my connection to the rest of the human race, I felt like I was dying, for some reason, and I didn't know why.'

Bruce Springsteen

THE ROCK CONNECTION

Rock is built entirely on bluster, myth and a revisionist approach to its own past which Stalin himself might regard as a bit heavy-handed. This means that anyone hoping to bluff their way through this strange and unpredictable world will have to slide everything up a gear. If they are especially daring, they can add to the great mound of bluffs the entire genre perches on, like putting a bean tin on the summit of Everest. Bruce Springsteen had this to say about the music business: 'Until I realised that rock music was my connection to the rest of the human race, I felt like I was dying, for some reason, and I didn't know why.'

The very essence of rock clings to a precise superficiality, presenting plastic statements and gestures as coming from a more honest, real and authentic place – seeing itself as the only place where such inauthentic authenticity can survive and flourish. This is the sort of dubious double-speak which thrives in this labyrinthine and synthetic world.

Rock fans are able to hold two utterly contradictory

views in their minds – that their music is simultaneously 'real' and equally 'unreal'. But to the outside world and to interlopers, they talk of albums and musicians in the hushed and reverential tones normally associated with great paintings and £5,000 bottles of Chateau Lafite Rothschild.

This book will give you all the ammunition you need to walk into that down-at-heel venue or back-street record shop where rock fans congregate and hold your own. It will conduct you safely through the main danger zones encountered in discussions about rock, and equip you with a vocabulary and evasive technique that will minimise the risk of being rumbled as a bluffer – it might even allow you to be accepted as a rock aficionado of rare knowledge and experience. But it will do more; it will give you the tools to impress legions of marvelling listeners with your wisdom and insight – without anyone discovering that, until you read it, you probably didn't know the difference between something called Limp Bizkit and a late-night bonding ritual in the public schools of England (involving biscuits).

So throw away those comfort-waist jeans and cushion-soled casuals and, while you're at it, toss that TV-advertised compilation album you got for Christmas into the recycling bin. We're going into the booming, beating, bogus heart of rock in all its many guises.

ROCK OF AGES

Rock is a mongrel genre with bits of assorted musical styles in its DNA. But like budget rhinoplasty, you can see the scars if you know where to look. Those who live and breathe rock like to present it as somehow being elemental, suggesting that it sprung forth from the earth fully formed. In reality, as much magpie as cuckoo, rock took what it wanted, evicted what it didn't want and dressed itself in the fineries of whatever it stole – as shall be seen.

BLUES, COUNTRY AND GOSPEL

Rock is obsessed with the past (things were more 'real' then) so always ensure that you talk about 'rock music's roots' as the first real musical melting pot in the 1950s – a meshing of black genres (rhythm and blues and gospel) with white ones (country and western).

While Elvis is the accepted 'King', bluffers should casually drop in the fact that Bill Haley pre-dates him and that the first rock 'n' roll single was 'Rocket 88' by

Jackie Brenston and His Delta Cats (which was really a pseudonym for Ike Turner's Kings of Rhythm).

The term 'rock 'n' roll' was a euphemism for, ahem, sexual congress and it is commonly accepted that it was popularised by 1950s American DJ Alan Freed who brought black music to white audiences at a time of segregation in the USA. His career was one marked by scandal; he was charged with inciting a riot in 1958 at a show in Boston and the next year was sacked by WABC-AM after the payola scandal (accepting bribes to promote certain records) engulfed the radio business. From this moment, rock 'n' roll really gained its outlaw status, breaking rules and refusing to behave with decorum.

ROBERT JOHNSON SELLS HIS SOUL

While Elvis was famously only filmed from the waist up initially on American TV (lest his wiggling legs and thrusting pelvis compromise the nation's morality), this, as all bluffers should know, was a mere bagatelle compared to blues legend Robert Johnson. The story goes that he was a very average blues guitarist and singer in the mid-1930s but took off like a rocket when, at a crossroads somewhere in Mississippi at midnight, he met the devil and had him tune his guitar and make him a master musician in a Faustian exchange for his soul.

Johnson, who died at 27 (*see* 'The 27 Club', page 101), left behind just a handful of recordings (and only a few photos of him exist), making him perhaps the most mythical and elusive figure in rock history. The fact that the devil/crossroads story is a load of hooey has not got in the way of the myth, and bluffers must solemnly nod and accept this as truth, thereby imbuing rock with a sense of satanic danger and netherworldly intrigue. He died, according to reports, after drinking a poisoned bottle of whisky handed to him by the irate husband of a woman he was propositioning for sex.

Thus the building blocks of rock were put in place – sex, the dark side, alcohol, immorality and lascivious behaviour. Johnson should consider himself lucky that Rasputin has not been dubbed the Godfather of Rock instead of him.

ELECTRIC GUITARS AND AMPLIFIERS

The devil, based on the Robert Johnson myth, has all the best tunes – but before rock music, they weren't very loud. Two technological advances combined to result in the parental cry that all bluffers must agree marked their childhood and adolescence – 'Turn that bloody racket down!'

The electric guitar dates back to the 1930s but came into its own in the 1950s. Two names, however, made it synonymous with rock – Les Paul, who is credited with creating the solid body electric guitar, and Gibson, whose mass-produced instruments pushed prices down and made them widely available. You might feel compelled to genuflect when either name is mentioned, eyes misting over as you rhapsodise about the 'action' of vintage Les Paul and Gibson guitars. The other guitar brand in the holy trinity is Fender, whose Telecaster and Stratocaster (always called 'Tele' and 'Strat' by seasoned bluffers) are perhaps the most iconic guitars of all time. Bruce Springsteen's default guitar is the Tele while Jimi Hendrix set fire to more Strats than Axl Rose has been late for concerts.

Such guitars are toothless, however, without amplifiers, and you will need to know the difference between the main brands of amps and be prepared to comment on one as offering superior sound.

Marshall amps are the most famous and most commonly used (Hendrix would drive his guitar through them like a spear on a regular basis), but connoisseur bluffers should proclaim their favourite to be the Vox, which was developed in Dartford (coincidentally the original home of The Rolling Stones) and was the brand used live by The Beatles after they signed an exclusive deal with the manufacturer to have them on stage. Another brand that you might mention is Orange, makers of amps such as those favoured by authentic rock legends Jimmy Page and Peter Green. If you want to bluff that extra mile, bone up on serial numbers and be prepared to talk about valves and 'roundness' of sound. If you want to go one further, quote Nigel Tufnel from the seminal rock spoof *This is Spinal Tap* and say about the volume dials on the band's amps 'these go to eleven'.

SUN STUDIO

Sam Phillips's Sun Studio in Memphis is both Mecca and Bethlehem to rock bluffers.

It opened in 1950 and was where 'Rocket 88' was recorded. It was the early studio of choice for not just Elvis but also Carl Perkins, Roy Orbison, Jerry Lee Lewis, Charlie Rich and Johnny Cash (the latter singer you will scramble to proclaim the most authentic and dangerous of the rock 'n' roll pioneers).

Records were 'cut' in the tiny studio, often in a single take. Its legendary status was cemented in 1953 when Elvis, then just 18, came in to record demo discs of 'My Happiness' and 'That's When Your Heartaches Begin' as a gift for his mother. He returned the following year to make more recordings and that was when Phillips spotted his huge commercial potential. 'If I could find a white man who had the Negro sound and the Negro feel,' Phillips is reported to have said in the decidedly un-PC language of the time, 'I could make a billion dollars.' He came close enough.

While Elvis in black leather in his 1968 comeback special on TV is his coolest image, and his Vegas years portly jumpsuit the one Elvis impersonators default to, it is Sun-era Elvis that the true bluffer will hold up as the best. For extra points, say that Elvis was never as good when he 'sold out' after RCA bought out his Sun contract in 1955 for $35,000.

DOO-WOP, SURF MUSIC AND THE 'IN-BETWEEN PERIOD'

Those with a sketchy grasp of rock's evolution assume that things went straight from Elvis to The Beatles, but the period between 1958 and 1962 is where you can talk meaningfully about 'lost periods', especially for Elvis, who did two years of military service between 1958 and 1960 and left the army as a sergeant in a tank battalion.

Post-Elvis 'doo-wop's' distinctive vocal harmonies, which had faded temporarily in popularity, swung back into vogue with New York's Brill Building (the training ground for songwriters Carole King, Neil Diamond, Neil Sedaka and others) churning out enormous hits in the genre for the likes of The Shirelles and The Crystals.

Concurrently, surf music pioneers like Link Wray and Dick Dale (as used in Quentin Tarantino movies), as well as Duane Eddy, used studio effects like reverb to create a tougher and more sinister sound. A direct line can be drawn here to The Beach Boys in the USA as well as The Shadows in the UK. You should confidently proclaim that doo-wop and surf music are the missing links in modern music and not just short-lived gimmicks.

Years before Margaret Thatcher and Ronald Reagan, it was rock music that forged the 'special relationship' between the UK and the USA.

THE BRITISH INVASION

Until this point, the USA had it all its own way, but the Brits wanted a piece of the action. The landmark moment is taken as The Beatles' first appearance on *The*

Ed Sullivan Show in February 1964, establishing the Holy Grail for all rock bands that followed in their wake – otherwise known as 'breaking America'.

The British invasion was initially a curiously northern English phenomenon. Alongside The Beatles were fellow Liverpudlians Gerry and The Pacemakers and The Searchers, as well as bands from Manchester (The Hollies, Herman's Hermits and Freddie and The Dreamers) and Newcastle (The Animals). London-based acts, notably The Rolling Stones and The Yardbirds, took a more bluesy approach but soon made their way across the Atlantic on the coat tails of their contemporaries.

The Animals in particular would have most enjoyed the 'coals to Newcastle' dynamic at play here as UK bands – obsessed with Delta blues, Sun-era rock 'n' roll and doo-wop – sold the music back to the country that invented it. Years before Margaret Thatcher and Ronald Reagan, it was rock music that forged the 'special relationship' between the UK and the USA.

DYLAN GOES ELECTRIC

The great myth about Bob Dylan was that he didn't 'plug in' until 1965, even though he had played in electric bands before moving to New York to make his name in the Greenwich Village folk scene.

The seismic moment of 'going electric' actually came in three parts. The first was 1965's *Bringing It All Back Home* album, split between acoustic and full band recordings. The second was his appearance at the Newport Folk Festival, where he had made his name in 1963 playing solo, as he and a full band plugged in for three songs (and from where came the apocryphal tale of folk overlord Pete Seeger being so enraged that he tried to cut the electricity supply with an axe mid-performance). The third was the 1966 world tour where Dylan would open the show solo and acoustic and then perform the second half with backing band The Hawks (later to rename themselves The Band).

All bluffers should know that the legendary cry of 'Judas!' by an audience member happened on 17 May 1966 at Manchester Free Trade Hall and not at the Royal Albert Hall in London ten days later (the venue mix-up was a result of a mislabelled bootleg recording).

Bluffers must say it was Dylan who turned pop (superficial, disposable) into rock (lyrically ambitious and 'profound'), forcing everyone, including The Beatles, to follow his lead.

GARAGE ROCK AND THE LEGACY OF *NUGGETS*

Garage rock was primarily a US phenomenon (so named as the bands rehearsed in garages) between 1963 and 1968. Retrospectively, it has been seen as gestating and nurturing punk – with its back-to-basics philosophy and championing of enthusiasm over competence – as well as psychedelic rock.

Key – and illustrative – recordings to know about are 'Louie, Louie' by The Kingsmen and 'Psychotic Reaction' by Count Five, with other leading lights being The Sonics, Paul Revere & The Raiders, The Chocolate Watchband, 13th Floor Elevators (featuring Roky

Erickson), The Nazz (featuring Todd Rundgren) and, er, The Golliwogs, featuring John Fogerty of Creedence Clearwater Revival.

The best of these recordings was compiled by Lenny Kaye (later to play guitar with Patti Smith) on the album *Nuggets: Original Artyfacts from the First Psychedelic Era, 1965–1968*. For many rock aficionados, the *Nuggets* boxset is as holy a relic as the Dead Sea Scrolls. Holier still is the *Pebbles* compilation that scooped up the obscurities that *Nuggets* missed – meaning all bluffers should say that while *Nuggets* is good, the real gems are to be found on *Pebbles*.

While rock 'n' roll started out as being all about singles, by the mid-1960s rock was all about the album.

THE ROCK CANON

Rock is deeply obsessed with its past and, more than that, the 'canon'. These are the absolutely essential recordings – the sacred cows of the form. Bluffers should not only be aware of them but also claim to own the original vinyl pressings of these key releases.

While rock 'n' roll started out as being all about singles, by the late 1960s rock was all about the album – a long-playing cohesive artistic statement that saw its apex (or, in many ways, its nadir) with the concept album and the double (best exemplified by The Beatles' *White Album*) or triple album. The longer the better is the rule of thumb for all bluffers here.

The majority of these albums were made in the mid-1960s to mid-1970s and almost exclusively by men. The bluffer must reconcile himself or herself to the sad fact that rock is 'men's business', often men in flares and cheesecloth shirts with long hair and/or beards.

Grouped by decade, there follow the essential albums every bluffer needs to have an opinion on, along with the non-obvious, little-heralded tracks you should claim are 'the most underrated' on the album, thereby suggesting you've waded through them all and know them better than you know your own family. Apologies if these rock milestones come in the form of a seemingly endless list, but that's the music business for you. If you ever had any doubt, just check out the latest 'charts'. Or if you don't know where to find them, visit Apple Music or Spotify for more lists than you could ever have dreamt possible in the early days of popular music.

Here you go. Take a deep breath and strap yourselves in. LET'S ROCK!

1960s

Blonde On Blonde – **Bob Dylan (1966)**

What to say Dylan goes to Nashville and creates the genre's first double album of spectral folk, country and rock, terming it 'that thin, that wild mercury sound'.

Bluffing tracks 'Visions of Johanna', 'Sad Eyed Lady of the Lowlands'.

Revolver – **The Beatles (1966)**

What to say Acid rock and pop collide in an album that pushed studio trickery to the outer limits with tape loops and electronics.

Bluffing tracks 'Tomorrow Never Knows', 'I'm Only Sleeping'.

Smile – **The Beach Boys (1966)**

What to say One of rock's legendary 'lost' milestones, this concept album was the intended follow-up to Pet Sounds. Enshrining a 'teenage symphony to God', it sadly booted principal songwriter Brian Wilson over the edge and only got an official release in 2011.
Bluffing tracks 'Heroes and Villains', 'Vega-Tables'.

The Velvet Underground & Nico – **The Velvet Underground & Nico (1967)**

What to say Andy Warhol, S&M and the nocturnal dystopia of Manhattan soundtracked by feedback, viola, Lou Reed's sneer and Nico's sepulchral vocals.
Bluffing tracks 'The Black Angel's Death Song', 'European Son (to Delmore Schwartz)'.

Disraeli Gears – **Cream (1967)**

What to say Eric Clapton's first 'supergroup' lassoes blues rock and psychedelia, accidentally inventing heavy metal and prog rock.
Bluffing tracks 'Tales of Brave Ulysses', 'SWLABR'.

Forever Changes – **Love (1967)**

What to say LA's best psychedelic band cook up a poisoned nightmare to kill the optimism of the Summer of Love.
Bluffing tracks 'The Red Telephone', 'Bummer in the Summer'.

Electric Ladyland – **Jimi Hendrix Experience (1968)**

What to say Third and final album with The Experience. Only hints at the new sounds that might have followed.

Bluffing tracks 'Burning of the Midnight Lamp', '1983 ... (a Merman I Should Turn to Be)'.

Astral Weeks – **Van Morrison (1968)**

What to say Normally a tedious blues-jazz tantrum in a hat, he lucked out in this unfurling folk and jazz dream letter about a Belfast idyll.
Bluffing tracks 'Slim Slow Slider', 'Cyprus Avenue'.

Kick Out The Jams – **MC5 (1968)**

What to say Detroit band caught live at their incendiary and polemic peak to the sound of the city falling apart. The line-up included two white men with absurd afros.
Bluffing tracks 'Rocket Reducer No. 62 (Rama Lama Fa Fa Fa)', 'Motor City is Burning'.

The Stooges – **The Stooges (1969)**

What to say Squalling and distorted guitars, the DNA of punk and nihilism courtesy of the man described by Alan Partridge as 'sweating lunatic Iggy Pop'.
Bluffing tracks 'We Will Fall', 'Real Cool Time'.

Trout Mask Replica – **Captain Beefheart and His Magic Band (1969)**

What to say The Ulysses of rock music, a wilfully unlistenable (and therefore 'amazing') stew of blues and free jazz.
Bluffing tracks 'Neon Meate Dream of a Octafish', 'My Human Gets Me Blues'.

1970s

Paranoid – Black Sabbath (1970)

What to say Horror metal from Birmingham and the Black Country with a guitarist who lost parts of two fingers; before Ozzy Osbourne became an MTV-approved cuddly gonk.

Bluffing tracks 'Planet Caravan', 'Rat Salad' (or should that be 'Bat'?).

There's A Riot Goin' On – Sly and The Family Stone (1971)

What to say Deranged on drugs and crippled by paranoia, Sly Stone swaps pop hits for fractured funk and soused soul about an imploding America.

Bluffing tracks 'Luv n' Haight', 'Africa Talks to You' 'The Asphalt Jungle'.

Pearl – Janis Joplin (1971)

What to say Released posthumously after hard living landed the final haymaker on her, Joplin rasps and wails until her lungs pop.

Bluffing tracks 'Buried Alive in the Blues', 'A Left Lonely'.

Electric Warrior – T. Rex (1971)

What to say Marc Bolan thro on ballet pumps to kick hi past into the bins round

Bluffing tracks 'M

Blue – **Joni Mitchell (1971)**

What to say Canadian Mitchell soars into another stratosphere and makes confessional folk rock the default setting of the 1970s.

Bluffing tracks 'River', 'A Case of You'.

The Rise And Fall Of Ziggy Stardust and The Spiders From Mars – **David Bowie (1972)**

What to say Bowie, after years of false starts, hits pay dirt by pretending to be the first rock star from outer space.

Bluffing tracks 'Five Years', 'Hang on to Yourself'.

Harvest – **Neil Young (1972)**

What to say Young's bucolic rock masterpiece about retreating to the country to whine about love, heroin, old farmers and (uh-oh) the days when women were dependent on men.

Bluffing tracks 'Are You Ready for the Country?', 'The Needle and The Damage Done'.

Transformer – **Lou Reed (1972)**

What to say Transvestism, heroin and references to *Land* from rock music's grumpiest man in pan ther.

Bluffing tracks 'Vicious', 'New York Telephone

Rolling Stones (1972)

uth of France while they is studiously ragged

blues as played by men taking time out from counting their millions.

Bluffing tracks 'Torn and Frayed', 'Shine a Light'.

Roxy Music – **Roxy Music (1972)**

What to say Bryan Ferry warbles and gargles in inimitable style as Brian Eno flies into the future on a box of wires.

Bluffing tracks 'Ladytron', 'If There is Something'.

The Dark Side Of The Moon – **Pink Floyd (1973)**

What to say A concept album about madness, greed and discord that pushed the notion of stereo sound and should have come with cigarette papers on the front. Mike Oldfield's *Tubular Bells* was usually standing by for some light relief.

Bluffing tracks 'Brain Damage', 'Breathe'.

New York Dolls – **New York Dolls (1973)**

What to say Cross-dressing, drug-fuelled sleazeballs teetering in high heels and smeared with lipstick, a decadent sham that effectively gave birth to both pu
and glam.

Bluffing tracks 'Pills', 'Jet Boy'.

Quadrophenia – **The Who (1973)**

What to say Not a concept album bu
a schizophrenic whose four pers
wait for it – the different me

Bluffing tracks 'I've
Godfather'.

Catch A Fire – **The Wailers (1973)**

What to say A giant Zippo lighter on the front suggested this was, ahem, a 'smoker's album' and made Bob Marley the first Third World megastar.
Bluffing tracks 'Slave Driver', 'Kinky Reggae'.

Band On The Run – **Paul McCartney and Wings (1973)**

What to say McCartney survived a mugging in Lagos to create an album to equal his best Beatles work and left John Lennon choking on his dust.
Bluffing tracks 'Let Me Roll it', 'Nineteen Hundred and Eighty-Five'.

Grievous Angel – **Gram Parsons (1974)**

What to say Posthumous release by pretty boy and wildman of country rock who put the Stones on a new course and whose drug-addled corpse was burned by friends in the Joshua Tree National Park as the young U2 took copious notes.
Bluffing tracks 'I Can't Dance', '$1000 Wedding'.

Physical Graffiti – **Led Zeppelin (1975)**

What to say The world's biggest band at the time ...uble album that ate the planet and birthed ...l babies.
... 'Custard Pie', 'The Rover'.

... (1975)

... roll jazz and the poetry of ...ack! It's better than it

Bluffing tracks 'Birdland', 'Land'.

Born To Run – Bruce Springsteen (1975)

What to say Bruce 'The Boss' Springsteen's magnum opus about running wild and, hey, just getting out of the rat race, baby.

Bluffing tracks 'Tenth Avenue Freeze-out', 'She's the One'.

A Night At The Opera – Queen (1975)

What to say Rococo, opulent, indulgent – a multi-tracked confection that will rot your teeth just by listening to it. Ludicrously brilliant and brilliantly ludicrous.

Bluffing tracks 'I'm in Love With My Car', 'Seaside Rendezvous'.

Ramones – Ramones (1976)

What to say Most songs are under two minutes long and are like comic books and B-movies set to guitars that sound like confused punk wasps.

Bluffing tracks 'I Don't Wanna Go Down to the Basement', 'Today Your Love, Tomorrow the World'.

Hotel California – Eagles (1976)

What to say Eighteen months in the making, this is the definitive 'cocaine California' soft rock album where the hotel is the indulgent metaphor for the music business ('You can check out anytime you like, but you can never leave').

Bluffing tracks 'Wasted Time', 'The Last Resort'.

Never Mind The Bollocks, Here's The Sex Pistols – Sex Pistols (1977)

What to say Bug-eyed Dickensian urchins declare unrelenting war on the UK, the royals, record labels, giving a stuff, etc., amid a tsunami of snot, sick and spit.
Bluffing tracks 'Bodies', 'Seventeen'.

Marquee Moon – Television (1977)

What to say The title track was ten minutes long and it involved different time signatures (!), improvisation (!!) and lengthy guitar solos (!!!) making it the Judas of New York punk.
Bluffing tracks 'Friction', 'Prove it'.

Bat Out Of Hell – Meat Loaf (1977)

What to say Both deadly serious and hilariously overblown, this album attempted to fuse Broadway, Wagner, Phil Spector, motorbikes and rock 'n' roll. Incredibly, it mostly succeeded.
Bluffing tracks 'All Revved Up With No Place to Go', 'For Crying Out Loud'.

Rumours – Fleetwood Mac (1977)

What to say The sound of the most expensive series of affairs, betrayals and bickering in history spilling out in an AOR (album-oriented rock) masterclass. Reinvented FM radio.
Bluffing tracks 'Go Your Own Way', 'Gold Dust Woman'.

Parallel Lines – Blondie (1978)

What to say Waving goodbye to the urine-flooded

floor of CBGB (*see* 'Live and Dangerous', page 75) punk, Blondie take over the world with new wave and disco.
Bluffing tracks 'One Way or Another', 'Fade Away and Radiate'.

Third/Sister Lovers – **Big Star (1978)**

What to say A big favourite with bluffers everywhere, Big Star's final album (in their first incarnation) is this most celebrated flawed 'masterpiece'. It's the one with the least number of actual tunes on it, and it's deep, confused and sad (and therefore 'important').
Bluffing tracks 'Holocaust', 'Kangaroo'.

London Calling – **The Clash (1979)**

What to say A punk band committing delicious heresy by releasing a double album (how indulgent!) about the paint blistering and peeling from the façade of the UK.
Bluffing tracks 'Four Horsemen', 'Clampdown'.

Metal Box – **Public Image Ltd (1979)**

What to say Sex Pistol Johnny Rotten reverts to John Lydon and drops the cartoon punk outrage for dub and post-punk experiments.
Bluffing tracks 'Albatross', 'Radio 4'.

Unknown Pleasures – **Joy Division (1979)**

What to say Slapstick music hall routines and novelty holiday sounds abound from Manchester mirthmeisters. Not really – it's darker than a crow's funeral.
Bluffing tracks 'Shadowplay', 'New Dawn Fades'.

1980s

Back In Black – **AC/DC (1980)**

What to say The metal album that swallowed the planet. New singer Brian Johnson makes their seaside postcard saucy lyrics rub shoulders with more elegiac themes in tribute to late vocalist Bon Scott.

Bluffing tracks 'Hells Bells', 'Let Me Put My Love Into You'.

PsychoCandy – **The Jesus and Mary Chain (1985)**

What to say Taking time out from creating riots at gigs, pipe cleaner-shaped Scots in black fuse The Stooges with The Beach Boys and The Ronettes. Impossible but true.

Bluffing tracks 'Taste The Floor', 'You Trip Me Up'.

The Queen Is Dead – **The Smiths (1986)**

What to say Whiny boo-hoo merchant Morrissey finally toughens up and windmills into the monarchy, old bosses, etc. with a boxing glove on the end of his quiff.

Bluffing tracks 'The Queen is Dead', 'Frankly, Mr Shankly'.

Hysteria – **Def Leppard (1987)**

What to say Despite the drummer losing an arm (an arm!), the Sheffield rockers make Bowie-inspired 'hair metal' the biggest radio sound in the world. Ripped jeans and vests become a global uniform for two years.

Bluffing tracks 'Love and Affection', 'Love Bites'.

Appetite For Destruction – **Guns N' Roses (1987)**

What to say Screeching and shirtless, Axl Rose and his hirsute band brought sleaze and swagger back to metal. It all got very un-PC and silly after this, though.
Bluffing tracks 'Rocket Queen', 'Out ta Get Me'.

The Joshua Tree – **U2 (1987)**

What to say Po-faced Irish 'conscience rockers' machine tool album designed to be lapped up by stadia the world over.
Bluffing tracks 'Red Hill Mining Town', 'One Tree Hill'.

Sign O' The Times – **Prince (1987)**

What to say Double album from nookie-obsessed psychedelic funk-rock homunculus about gender, religion and AIDS. A thousand times more fun than it sounds.
Bluffing tracks 'The Ballad of Dorothy Parker', 'The Cross'.

Doolittle – **Pixies (1989)**

What to say Boston band invents quiet-loud-quiet rock dynamic (later 'borrowed' by Nirvana) in songs about environmental catastrophe, numerology, the Bible and sliced eyeballs. Yuck.
Bluffing tracks 'No 13 Baby', 'Dead'.

The Stone Roses – **The Stone Roses (1989)**

What to say Hapless goths discover The Byrds and rave drugs and, along with Happy Mondays, create Madchester dance-rock. Vertiginously diminishing returns ever since.
Bluffing tracks 'I Am the Resurrection', 'This is the One'

1990s

Nevermind – **Nirvana (1991)**

What to say Grunge benchmark that actually had more in common with 1970s AOR with added screaming and existential tantrums from men dressed like Dorothy's scarecrow.

Bluffing tracks 'Territorial Pissings', 'Stay Away'.

Metallica – **Metallica (1991)**

What to say Enormously dysfunctional thrash metal band become even more dysfunctional arena band singing about how everything's gone wrong and it's not fair.

Bluffing tracks 'Sad But True', 'The Unforgiven'.

Loveless – **My Bloody Valentine (1991)**

What to say Tunes and melodies get bullied out of town by washes of feedback and drones. Bluffers will nod sagely and say it's 'demanding' (it is) but 'rewarding' (eventually).

Bluffing tracks 'Soon', 'Only Shallow'.

Ten – **Pearl Jam (1991)**

What to say Grunge's other blockbuster album. It traded Nirvana's blankness and nihilism for bellowed everyman emoting about Very Significant Topics like school shootings and dark family secrets.

Bluffing tracks 'Black', 'Porch'.

Automatic For The People – R.E.M. (1992)

What to say Wherein college rock egghead Michael Stipe gives up on mumbled 'esoteric' vocals and writes huge radio smashes about being a bit sad.

Bluffing tracks 'Find the River', 'Nightswimming'.

Grace – Jeff Buckley (1994)

What to say Son of Tim, this is Jeff's only 'proper' album before he drowned in 1997. Effectively paved the way for Radiohead (Mark II), Muse, Coldplay, Snow Patrol, etc., but don't hold that against him.

Bluffing tracks 'Lilac Wine', 'Eternal Life'.

Definitely Maybe – Oasis (1994)

What to say Before they became a self-parodying laughing stock, the Gallagher brothers spun parochial daydreaming of rock stardom into Britpop gold.

Bluffing tracks 'Slide Away', 'Columbia'.

Odelay – Beck (1996)

What to say Smart-arse would-be-Prince-style magazine stoner prince Beck decides to finally write some songs. World is amazed.

Bluffing tracks 'Hotwax', 'The New Pollution'.

OK Computer – Radiohead (1997)

What to say An enormous yowl about how machines are taking over and the Millennium Bug would explode the world. They were half right but stopped writing 'songs' in a huff after millions of people liked this.

Bluffing tracks 'Let Down', 'Electioneering'.

2000s

Rated R – **Queens Of The Stone Age (2000)**

What to say Stoner rock with riffs the size of the Great Wall of China and lyrics about drugs, taking drugs and drug paranoia. Plus more drugs just to be sure.

Bluffing tracks 'Leg of Lamb', 'Monsters in the Parasol'.

White Blood Cells – **The White Stripes (2001)**

What to say Guitar, drums and elemental blues howling from futurephobic Jack White with added 'wheeze' about pretending his drumming ex-wife was his sister.

Bluffing tracks 'Little Room', 'The Same Boy You've Always Known'.

Is This It – **The Strokes (2001)**

What to say Deliberately nonchalant pretty and posh public school boys play dress-up with New York punk history and bowl both indie dictators and style magazines over.

Bluffing tracks 'The Modern Age', 'Soma'.

A Rush Of Blood To The Head – **Coldplay (2002)**

What to say With Radiohead busy making unlistenable music, Coldplay cleaned up with songs that vaguely hint at universal themes of love and redemption but actually make no sense.

Bluffing tracks 'Clocks', 'Amsterdam'.

Permission To Land – The Darkness (2003)

What to say Meta-ironic take on bombastic rock and hair metal by Lowestoft (Lowestoft!) rockers in catsuits and tongues in each other's cheeks.

Bluffing tracks 'Friday Night', 'Growing on Me'.

Funeral – Arcade Fire (2004)

What to say The world's most humourless band write sad songs about hope in an uncaring world and become Canadian superstars despite dressing like extras in *Little House on the Prairie*.

Bluffing tracks 'Une Année Sans Lumière', 'Haïti'.

American Idiot – Green Day (2004)

What to say An overblown rock opera about an anti-hero who thinks Americans are stupid – a bit like *The Catcher in the Rye* with studded belts, tattoos and spiked hair. Hilariously also became a musical.

Bluffing tracks 'City of the Damned', 'Give Me Novacaine'.

Black Holes and Revelations – Muse (2006)

What to say Enormously well versed in prog-rock bombast, Queen-style pantomime and conspiracy theories, Muse did the impossible by becoming more adorably ludicrous than Radiohead.

Bluffing tracks 'Exo-Politics', 'Map of the Problematique'.

Whatever People Say I Am, That's What I'm Not – Arctic Monkeys (2006)

What to say Precocious Sheffield rockers create a loose concept album around a day in the 21st-century life of equally blank and clued-up teens with ferocious erudition.

Bluffing tracks 'From the Ritz to the Rubble', 'A Certain Romance'.

Only By The Night – Kings Of Leon (2008)

What to say Southern rock brothers (and cousin) polish boogie rock to a U2-level stadium sheen and attract huge audiences and cries of 'sell-out' despite not seeking medical help about 'your sex is on fire'.

Bluffing tracks 'Crawl', 'Manhattan'.

2010s

The Rolling Stones are proof that cartoon decadence is somehow admirable among men who waved goodbye to their 20s half a century ago.

El Camino – The Black Keys (2011)

What to say They took The White Stripes' musical triptych (voice, guitar, drums) and went deliberately widescreen by getting in dance (not rock!) producer

Dangermouse to give it more scope and a bit more groove. And added in more instruments, the sneaks.
Bluffing tracks 'Lonely Boy', 'Gold On The Ceiling'.

Lonerism – **Tame Impala (2012)**

What to say Australian psych-slash-glam-rockers replace most of the guitars with synths to make an album that sounds like going potholing through Spotify after a limitless buffet of mind-altering drugs. Probably best not to try this at home.
Bluffing tracks 'Elephant', 'Feels Like We Only Go Backwards'.

Days Are Gone – **Haim (2013)**

What to say Three hipster LA sisters try to recalibrate *Rumours* by Fleetwood Mac for the 2010s and it mostly comes off. Californian band X California rock lodestone = soft rock bombast in excelsis.
Bluffing tracks 'Don't Save Me', 'Forever'

... Like Clockwork – **Queens Of The Stone Age (2013)**

What to say A more 'considered' approach to narcotic abandon sees the desert rockers reborn and everything snapping back into focus with a pulsing and creeping vibe that still manages to boogie.
Bluffing tracks 'I Sat By The Ocean', 'If I Had A Tail'.

AM – **Arctic Monkeys (2013)**

What to say Yorkshire teens reach a type of maturity and drew in Josh Homme from Queens Of The Stone

Age (him again) who taught these young dogs new tricks about how to make a muscular and soulful vibe as important as the songs.

Bluffing tracks 'R U Mine', 'Why'd You Only Call Me When You're High?'

Songs Of Innocence – U2 (2014)

What to say The band wanted it to be their most listened to album ever but it became their most deleted after a deal with Apple saw it rammed unbidden into the collection of every iTunes user in the world. Despite the backlash, Bono's quest for ubiquity continues apace.

Bluffing tracks 'The Miracle (Of Joey Ramone)', 'Every Breaking Wave'.

Royal Blood – Royal Blood (2014)

What to say Like The White Stripes and The Black Keys, except this British duo swapped the guitar for a bass that is tricked out to sound like a guitar playing a thousand thundering Led Zeppelin riffs simultaneously. Four strings, it seems, can be better than six.

Bluffing tracks 'Out Of The Black', 'Figure It Out'.

Lost In The Dream – The War On Drugs (2014)

What to say Cinematic and mournful, the Philadelphia indie rockers create a beautifully washed-out album that mixes Americana with Eighties rock. Amazingly it still succeeds despite occasionally sounding like Dire Straits without the headbands.

Bluffing tracks 'Red Eyes', 'Under The Pressure'.

Sometimes I Sit And Think, And Sometimes I Just Sit – Courtney Barnett (2015)

What to say Australian slacker/rocker's debut album is bursting at the seams with hooks and sharp observations on the minutiae of life, finding the profound in the quotidian, combining witty tongue twisters with arresting blasts of grunge.

Bluffing tracks 'Elevator Operator', 'Depreston'.

Joy As An Act Of Resistance – Idles (2018)

What to say Bristolian rabble-rousers deliver a type of politicised and incandescent rock that is purifying and uplifting despite the world around them being permanently on the brink of collapse. A soundtrack to counter the toxic side of Brexit.

Bluffing tracks 'Danny Nedelko', 'Colossus'.

B

A mummy's boy truck driver from Tupelo, Mississippi, Elvis was the first accepted superstar (read: white) face of rock 'n' roll.

THE CLASSIC BLUFFS

Picking the greatest rock acts in history is a risky business for bluffers: go too mainstream and face being dismissed as an arriviste with obvious taste; go too obscure and risk being asked questions about them that you have no answers for.

The obvious solution is to choose the greatest rock bluffers of all time – those acts and bands which continually reinvented themselves and actually achieved the rocky heights to which you aspire. The following masters of their art were, and in many cases still are, among the most accomplished bluffers in rock history. You should kneel at their feet and pay due homage.

ELVIS PRESLEY

A mummy's boy truck driver from Tupelo, Mississippi, Elvis was the first accepted superstar (read: white) face of rock 'n' roll. There are seven ages of Elvis that every bluffer needs to know about:

- the Sun Years Elvis (remember that Sun was his first record label);
- the Army Years Elvis (when he served in Germany and released nothing);
- the Hollywood Elvis (making at least ten of the worst films of all time), at a stage in his career when his 'forceful' manager, 'Colonel' Tom Parker, an illegal Dutch immigrant, wouldn't let him leave the country on the grounds that he (Parker) would be deported on returning to the USA;
- the 1968 Comeback Special Elvis (dressed in black leather);
- the Getting Fat in Graceland Elvis;
- the Sweating on Stage in Vegas to Pay the Bills Elvis (featuring rhinestones and chest-and-paunch-exposing jumpsuits);
- and the Dead on the Toilet Elvis. Bluffers must pick just one as their favourite and unwaveringly defend it to the death. He's not dead, of course. Everyone knows that.

CHUCK BERRY

Born in 1926, the duck-walking, law-breaking, armed-robbing, prison-serving, ding-a-ling-proffering singer and guitarist, amazingly made it to the ripe old age of 90, playing regularly well into his mid-80s. Along with Little Richard, he was one of the first real showmen of the rock 'n' roll era and a black superstar in an age when the media still segregated and wanted 'palatable' white faces to front this youth sound. Scandals (notably covertly filming women on the toilet) turned him into a tragic figure rather than a renegade. Berry is very easy for bluffers to pretend to know all about – just hear one of his songs ('Johnny B Goode' or 'No Particular Place to Go' are the big ones) and if you vaguely whistle it, you can claim it's any of his songs.

THE BEATLES

The alpha and omega of rock for bluffers, they did everything, did it first and (mostly) did it best. Pepped up on speed pills in Hamburg dives, they returned to Liverpool and manager Brian Epstein homogenised them into loveable moptops and made them stars. Just seven years in the public eye, their career is like the 1960s on fast-forward, racing from black and white (the early years of Beatlemania) and exploding into colour (mid-1960s acid years, *Sgt Pepper, Magical Mystery Tour*) before falling apart in a stew of acrimony, envy, distrust, money, bad financial decisions, drugs and beards ('Let it Be', *Abbey Road*). Different bluffers will pick a different Beatle as their favourite: Paul (seems music hall, actually avant-garde); John (coruscating and hypocritical hippie but the erudite choice); George (the spiritual choice); and Ringo (the double-bluff comedy choice).

The alpha and omega of rock for bluffers, The Beatles did everything, did it first and (mostly) did it best.

BOB DYLAN

'I've got my Bob Dylan mask on,' said the erstwhile Robert Zimmerman at a Halloween show in 1964. Dylan really is the patron saint of bluffers; he adopts a persona and an image to suit his needs, sneeringly sidestepping any attempts to call his bluff. First there was the folk singer and protest singer (bluffing his way as the new Woody Guthrie), the drug-fried, acid-rocking, speed-poet (French symbolist poet in Carnaby Street threads), the country-living family man, the lost and angry divorcee, the born-again Christian, the utterly awful 1980s, the minor rebirth in the 1990s as he faced his own mortality, before ultimately being condemned to tour eternally as the direct descendant of the itinerant folk minstrel he first pretended to be. Dylan is a warning from history about how if you bluff, and the blowin' wind changes, your face will stay that way.

THE WHO

After starting off as a west London mod band, success in the USA quickly turned them into bloated rock caricatures where they (or rather drummer Keith Moon) wrote the lazy rule book of rock excess (blowing things up, 'hilariously' dressing up as a Nazi, driving a car into a swimming pool, being permanently drunk/on drugs), rotten misogyny (attacking his wife) and dying from it all. Pete Townshend will continually have to face up to the embarrassment of, now in his pension years, writing the youth rebellion cry of 'I hope I die before I get old' and churning out enormously indulgent rock operas about schizophrenia (*Quadrophenia*) and deaf, dumb and blind pinball players (*Tommy*).

THE ROLLING STONES

From Dartford, an otherwise unremarkable town at the lower end of Greater London's alimentary canal, they have for well over 50 years now (with assorted personnel changes) played the bluff that they are old, black bluesmen, despite (Sir) Mick Jagger (now a great-grandfather) studying at the LSE and Keith 'Keef' Richards demonstrating an inexcusable fondness for pirate headbands. As such, most rock bluffers love them as they have 'survived' (apart from Brian Jones who drowned) and are proof that cartoon decadence is somehow admirable among men who waved goodbye to their 20s half a century ago. They started off pretending to be a blues band, suddenly became amazing from 1965 to 1969 and then settled into becoming a slowly unfurling parody of themselves – in terms of both music and 'lifestyle'.

THE BYRDS

Initially America's attempt to 'make a Beatles' of their own (they did it far better with The Monkees), The Byrds were arguably the first 'scenester' band and, as such, should be clasped tightly to the bosom of any bluffer as kindred spirits. Their breakthrough came through a series of Dylan covers (bluffers covering King Bluffer = bluff cubed). They soon tired of the hit singles so tried to spook everyone by 'going psychedelic' (again The Monkees did it better with the *Head* movie) and then, sniffing the denim and moustaches on the breeze at the turn into the 1970s, went 'country rock'. Three very different bands in less than half a decade? That's like winning gold, silver and bronze at the Bluffers' Olympics.

EAGLES

Seeing what The Byrds, Gram Parsons, Neil Young and others had done with country and rock, Eagles (there is no definitive article in their name) were perhaps the first career rockers and, as such, should have a little shrine built to them by bluffers the world over. They went stratospheric with 'Hotel California' and then fell out, swearing only to re-form 'if Hell freezes over'. Later, inevitably, they re-formed and called their reunion the Hell Freezes Over tour, displaying the kind of steel-jawed chutzpah the average bluffer can only dream of.

LED ZEPPELIN

Made the 1970s entirely theirs by 'borrowing' heavily from the blues, showing what a poker-faced bluff can really deliver. Singer and lyricist Robert 'the Golden God' Plant created a parallel universe of marauding Vikings ('Hammer of the Gods'), mysticism ('Kashmir') and pixies and elves and whatnot ('The Battle of Evermore') – while all the time being a skinny bloke from the Black Country in giant bell-bottoms and a skimpy silk blouse. This, combined with the band's simultaneous indulgence in the debauchery and excess of a touring lifestyle, which set the infamously base standards for all who followed, is the reason rock bluffers recognise in Zeppelin a paradigm of a super-bluff played with staggering aplomb. But, to be fair, they did have Jimmy Page – which gave them something of an advantage.

JIMI HENDRIX

The bluffer's choice as greatest guitarist and greatest rock star of all time, Hendrix was mixed-race (African-American, European and Cherokee) and did military service before reinventing himself as a guitar-torching dandy peacock when he moved to London and made everything else old hat. His career was short-lived, but phosphorous, mixing covers of Dylan and The Beatles, as well as his own songs that syphoned in jazz and blues and spat out heavy metal. You can earn extra points by saying that, when he lived in London (just off Hanover Square), his flat was next door to where Handel lived over 200 years earlier. You can now visit a twin-themed museum dedicated to both in the actual buildings they inhabited.

PINK FLOYD

There are two ages of Pink Floyd, and bluffers, just as with The Beatles and Elvis, have to decide which side of the fence they want to stand on. There are the Syd Barrett Years when they were the psychedelic mind-bending kings of the London freakbeat scene, singing about oddballs stealing washing ('Arnold Layne') and dark nursery rhymes ('See Emily Play'), and creating space rock ('Interstellar Overdrive'). Then there are the post-Syd years (aka The Enormously Successful Concept Album Years) where they wrote long cycle works about madness (*The Dark Side of the Moon*) or how nasty teachers at their expensive schools were beastly to them (*The Wall*).

KISS

Such bluffers that they hid behind face paint and pretended they were the devil incarnate (Gene Simmons), a starchild (Paul Stanley), a spaceman (Ace Frehley) or, erm, a cat (Peter Criss). Given that their music was desperately limp (a Pot Noodle version of what the New York Dolls did), they relied on dressing up, Halloween stage props (eating blood capsules) and explosions to detract from their numerous musical shortcomings. There are lessons to be learned here for any aspiring bluffers. In rock especially, drawing attention to a gaudy and brash surface allows you to hide the fact that there's very little else in the tank.

BLACK SABBATH

Lead singer Ozzy Osbourne used to work in a slaughterhouse in Birmingham, while guitarist Tommy Iommi lost the tops of two of his fingers in a factory accident – and their music sounds exactly like that. Lots of references to black magic and the devil (lifted from budget horror movies) gave the band a dangerous reputation they barely warranted. Exemplary bluffers.

AC/DC

Despite being seen as the heavyweight champions of heavy metal, they are really just a very loud blues band with a puerile preoccupation with innuendo (excessive single entendre) and a diminutive lead guitarist who looks like he escaped from the pages of *The Beano* (or, more accurately, given his Scottish heritage, the adopted brother of Wee Jimmy Krankie). They are, however, enormously good fun and, like Chuck Berry, all their songs are basically the same so bluffers can confidently claim to be well versed in both the Bon Scott era (all of the 1970s) and the Brian Johnson era too (1980 onwards). Johnson, however, left the band in 2016 due to hearing issues only to be replaced on the road by Axl Rose (but he may still return).

DAVID BOWIE

Rock music's biggest chameleon and, hence, biggest bluffer. He had so many false starts before he got famous with *Ziggy Stardust* (mod, acid rocker, hippie, space hippie) that he felt that changing with every album was part of his DNA. So throughout the 1970s he raided a new dressing-up box for each album and pretty much nailed each new reincarnation. The speed of change, however, was like a runaway train and from the 1980s onwards it was more guff than gold (the ghastly

Tin Machine project, the *Labyrinth* film, 'Dancing in the Street' with that other old imposter Mick Jagger, and a drum and bass album). He sadly passed away in January 2016, with his final two albums (*The Next Day* and *Blackstar*) ranking among his career highs.

Bowie was rock music's biggest chameleon and, hence, biggest bluffer. He had so many false starts before he got famous with *Ziggy Stardust* (mod, acid rocker, hippie, space hippie) that he felt that changing with every album was part of his DNA.

SEX PISTOLS

Created by Malcolm McLaren to whip up easy controversy (songs vaguely calling for anarchy or else saying the Queen was a bit rubbish – as well as inevitably expletive-studded TV appearances). The band's biggest bluff was that they were trying to destroy rock 'n' roll (covers of songs by The Who, The Monkees and The Stooges show they were keen students of the past). Really they were just having a laugh and hoping to make 'cash from [predictable] chaos' – an admirable pursuit for any bluffer.

THE CLASH

Seen as the 'social conscience' of British punk, the band talked in broken allegories and buzzwords (like 'riot' and 'war') and tried to smash the past ('No Elvis, Beatles or The Rolling Stones in 1977' they sang, despite sounding like all three of them). They even made double and triple albums (making them just as prog as the rock they were supposedly in opposition to) and, after they split, let their music be used in ads to sell jeans and British Airways flights.

THE SMITHS

Like Bob Dylan, Smiths' singer Morrissey created a character that eventually became a masquerade. Wearing a permanent mask normally risks having your face eaten by it, but Morrissey's enormous chin saved him from being fitted with one that was too tight. He became a living god for many while singing about how no one liked him/wanted him/understood him. Morrissey's unpalatable political pronouncements in recent years have alienated him from all but his most loyal/deluded fans – making him the boy who called bluff too often.

U2

Among the greatest bluffers in the entire bluff-blighted history of rock (what else can you call a band whose guitarist styles himself preposterously as 'The Edge'?). On paper they are great humanitarians, and no doubt they mean well in their own somewhat self-serving way. Their critics say that they are money-minting Celtic-brand proselytisers; their admirers say that they are one of the world's great exponents of 'arena' rock with some equally great anthems. Take your pick, but you can't help but feel that diminutive lead singer Bono's suspiciously built-up shoes are a metaphor for a band that professes to have lofty ideals, but in fact comes up a bit short. The backlash against the disastrous release of *Songs Of Innocence*, the album they dropped in everyone's iTunes collection in 2014, was proof they couldn't even give their music away.

NIRVANA

Like Morrissey, Kurt Cobain became indescribably famous and loved for singing songs about being an unloved, 'negative creep'. His low self-esteem might have stemmed from an earlier career as a janitor at the school that he had dropped out of. Managing to bluff his way to becoming the world's most famous, and most miserable, rock star from such unpromising beginnings was an extraordinary achievement. But the fame/self-loathing contradiction was something he was not prepared for or able to handle, so he sought comfort in heroin and, when that wasn't enough, he killed himself.

OASIS

A two-headed, always-fighting, sibling-rivalling Beatles karaoke machine. Debut album *Definitely Maybe* had an arrogance and a swagger that detracted from the fact that not much was happening under the bonnet. By the time the second album was released, the bluff was being spread wafer thin, but still they whipped it along, becoming simply enormous. By then it was too late to stop and the machine kept the plates spinning. After that the bluff, for all its bluster, became quite funny so they kept going. Then it stopped being funny and, as a warning to bluffers everywhere, they pushed the pretence too far over several more albums even though their pants were down. They split in 2009 and (so far) have resisted offers to re-form.

RADIOHEAD

The connoisseur bluffer's choice, but one fraught with danger. You can't say you like early Radiohead, as the breakthrough single 'Creep' is regarded as a millstone by the band. Saying you like *The Bends* and *OK Computer* means you have opted for 'easy Radiohead' when they wrote songs that had tunes that lots of people actually liked. Saying you like *Kid A*, *Amnesiac*, *In Rainbows* and *The King of Limbs* seems like the hardest bluff – as these are albums their fans treat as holy relics and dissect for hidden meaning and praise the difficult nature of their sound – but the reality is that you can just whistle any old nonsense and it'll sound like something from these albums. Easy.

THE STROKES

They managed to convince the world they were skinny urchins from the underbelly of Manhattan, wrapped in the mythology of CBGB. In reality they were privately educated at some of Europe and America's most expensive schools – hell of a bluff. It's not a good idea to get caught up in rock arguments about 'authenticity' (the biggest bluff anyone in rock can pull off); instead admire their audacity. The fact that their debut album (*Is This It*) was a breath of fresh air after years of ghastly American sports metal (*see* Limp Bizkit, etc., page 65) negates any arguments about whether or not they were 'real' or if they 'meant it' (things you should pretend to care about).

THE WHITE STRIPES

Arriving at the same time as The Strokes, Detroit two-piece The White Stripes were hooked into notions of a 'new rock revival'. But while The Strokes looked back to New York in the 1970s, The White Stripes looked further back – to the bluesmen of the 1930s and 1940s. A stripped-down sound of guitars, drums and Jack White's alley-cat voice were all they needed to kick up a blues rock storm, dressing in uniform (only clothes coloured red, white and black were permissible) to symbolise their minimalism, and built a whole mythology around themselves especially regarding whether they were married (they were, but divorced), brother and sister (they weren't) or both (eewww!). Bluffers can learn from this – keep your bluff simple, structured and never step out of character. Keep your audience guessing, and never feel the need to explain.

COLDPLAY

Coldplay took the sound of Radiohead and the broad brushstroke sincerity of U2 and beat both at their own game. They are confessional rock without any of the confession, hinting at big emotions but not actually going there, presenting ill-structured lyrics as intense meditations on the fragility of the human condition, all wrapped up in the kind of choruses that should come with a free lighter to hold up in the stadium (except that it might be 'bad for the environment').

ARCTIC MONKEYS

Precocious alternative rockers coming out of Sheffield like a combination of The Strokes, John Cooper Clark and George Formby, they exploded quickly and, for the most part, have managed to sustain it, evolving with each album. This is probably because they are keen to forget the time they were spoken of in the same breath as Kaiser Chiefs and The Cribs. Alex Turner was, from the off, a highly literate songwriter, leading to accusations he was getting help from music's older associates with his lyrics (he wasn't); so he is one of the few rock stars accused of bluffing who was quickly able to vindicate themselves.

Some sub-genres are complementary, but others are natural enemies (like mods and rockers, indie kids and metal fans, punks and prog fans, teddy boys and, well, anyone who likes anything that happened after the 1950s).

GENNING UP ON GENRES

Saying you are a fan of rock will only get you so far, especially when a serious rock fan (or another bluffer) challenges you and asks you what kind of rock you like. Some sub-genres are complementary, but others are natural enemies (like mods and rockers, indie kids and metal fans, punks and prog fans, teddy boys and, well, anyone who likes anything that happened after the 1950s). You will need an overview of the main genres that sit within the rock cluster so that you can back up your initial bluff about understanding and appreciating rock, with a sub-bluff about which of its many strains really floats your boat.

BLUES ROCK

Originating in the early to mid-1960s, this is essentially 12-bar blues, but amplified. Acts like The Rolling Stones and The Yardbirds cut their teeth on this music, but very quickly it collapsed and ate itself with lots of guitar soloing and 'jamming'. Here technical ability becomes prized over and above 'feeling', and the wise bluffer should back slowly out of the room when talk turns to 'pentatonic scales' and 'blue notes' – not because you can't bluff your way out of a cul-de-sac, but because the subject matter is very boring.

Acts like Jefferson Airplane, the Grateful Dead and early Pink Floyd are typical of the genre that also relied on strobe lighting and oil-wheel projections to cover up the fact that the performers were so off-the-planet they couldn't break out of a chord cycle for up to seven hours.

PSYCHEDELIC ROCK

This is what happened when rock music discovered hallucinogenic drugs and simultaneously stumbled on drones (a monotonously repeated tone) and ragas (a distinctively melodic mode, also repeated), most commonly associated with Indian music. The exciting cross-cultural movement also featured British and American musicians incapable of holding a sitar the right way up for their groundbreaking early albums. Acts like Jefferson Airplane, the Grateful Dead and early Pink Floyd are typical of the genre that also relied on strobe lighting and oil-wheel projections to cover up the fact that the performers were so off-the-planet they couldn't break out of a chord cycle for up to seven hours.

SOUTHERN ROCK

Developed, as the name suggests, in the southern states of the USA in the 1970s. Perhaps the hairiest of all rock sub-genres – a middle parting was compulsory as was a moustache the size of a wholemeal loaf. Typified by the Allman Brothers Band and the mostly late Lynyrd Skynyrd (whose 'Free Bird' is the genre's anthem and, when played live, ideally runs for a fortnight). Warning: contains dangerous levels of denim, belts with Confederate flag buckles, 'boogie', and lyrics which frequently feature something known as the 'rebel yell' (which has nothing to do with the 1983 Billy Idol album of the same name).

PROG ROCK

Short for 'progressive rock', this genre tried to intellectualise a genre that was, for the most part, about dumb fun. Bluffers need to approach with extreme caution, as its most belligerent fans will want to get into lengthy discussions about convoluted lyrical references to the classical world, as well as time signatures so complex they would stun a cuckoo clock. Exponents of prog rock (like Yes, Genesis and post-Syd Pink Floyd) were often university educated, steeped in classical music, and wanted rock music to be venerated in the same way as Wagner or Bach were. It meant that 'suites' replaced songs and tracks, while albums and concerts lasted longer than the summer holidays.

SOFT ROCK

Not an oxymoron, but a conscious attempt to have rock music more in keeping with pop – so there was an emphasis on big choruses and a shiny and lush production sound that made it appear fuller and cleaner than rock, which was more obsessed with the dirt under its own fingernails. Say that it hit its peak in the 1970s with acts like Elton John, the Carpenters, Chicago and Supertramp. Like rock, it had guitars, but they were often turned down and made 'polite' with pianos featuring heavily (though not 'heavily' in the volume sense). It was also known as 'adult contemporary', as it was the kind of music your parents or teachers might play to pretend they were still 'in touch'.

GLAM

This is where rock discovered a sense of fun and androgyny, just as it threatened to settle into a very serious, very male, very pretentious, and very heterosexual orthodoxy. The emphasis was on men dressing up in flamboyant clothes and make-up (it was also known as 'glitter rock' in the USA) and playing with uninhibited sexuality. Marc Bolan's reinvention of his pixie folk band Tyrannosaurus Rex into the glamorous T. Rex in 1971 (*see* 'Rock Fashion and Tribes', page 67) is seen as the real starting point and soon the charts were invaded by Ziggy-era genuinely talented musicians like Bowie, Roxy Music and Lou Reed. It quickly got spoiled by the 'bricklayers in drag' acts that tried to reinvent themselves and cash in, but it was fun while it lasted.

Metal celebrates being loud, dumb and generally lacking in musical merit.

METAL

The unavoidable genre's origins are disputed but bluffing tracks in its development include 'You Really Got Me' by The Kinks, anything by Jimi Hendrix, and 'Born to be Wild' by Steppenwolf (which included the phrase 'heavy metal thunder'). At heart it is merely blues rock played louder and a bit faster, but following in the wake of Black Sabbath, Deep Purple and Led Zeppelin, it became associated with motorbikes, denim, leather and a cartoonish obsession with the occult. Despite being camp (hilariously so at times), its calling card is machismo and, despite a teenage-like obsession with anything phallic, a vigorous heterosexuality that also stands at odds with the long hair and, later, lipstick. It celebrates being loud, dumb and generally lacking in musical merit and, as such, should have a special place in a bluffer's collection.

PUNK

You will come to a crossroads here in regard to which 'punk' to choose. There is American punk which, chronologically, came first with acts like The Velvet Underground, The Stooges and MC5 in the late 1960s leading to the New York Dolls and then the CBGB (*see* 'Live and Dangerous', page 75) bands such as the Ramones, Television and Blondie, and was often about blankness, apoliticism and nihilism. There is also British punk, which sprung out of pub rock and led to bands like The Damned (which released the first UK punk single, 'New Rose'), Sex Pistols and The Clash, which took on a vague and somewhat amateurish political agenda. Which one you choose will require different bluffing skills and the ability to attack the other punk as not being 'real punk'.

NEW WAVE

Like punk, it has a USA/UK split in its origins, but most accepted histories suggest it emerged in Britain in the first aftershock of punk in the mid- to late 1970s. It drew on a wider musical pool – incorporating ska, funk, reggae and dub, and utilised synthesisers. If you're caught short and unsure if a band is punk or new wave, you should hold your nerve and simply describe them as 'kind of punk-into-new-wave', as no one knows exactly where the dividing line is.

NEW WAVE OF BRITISH HEAVY METAL

Happening at the same time as new wave, NWOBHM (as it was acronymically and unpronounceably known) was partly influenced by both glam and punk which, ironically, both contributed to the leading lights of metal falling out of fashion. In that sense, it was revivalist but was able to reconcile this with elements of the music that slayed the metal dinosaurs' antecedents. Are you following so far? Being able to hold two contradictory notions in your head at the same time is something bluffers should be in awe of and so NWOBHM acts like Iron Maiden, Def Leppard and Saxon should have your unfettered admiration.

SPEED METAL/THRASH

Heavy metal for those who feel that normal heavy metal isn't fast or crunchy enough. The genre is dominated by what has, over the years, come to be known as The Big Four – Metallica, Anthrax, Slayer and Megadeth. All have logos (when it comes to thrash, logos are as important as the music) that look like they were cut from sheet metal and, in many ways, they were. Songs are characterised by guttural singing (like a horse being punched in the chest), 'shredding' (guitar solos that go 'widdly-widdly-widdly' at speeds approaching 800mph) and lyrics about how the system, you know, is just keeping the kids down.

GOTH

It's Halloween every day of the year for goths who dress entirely in black (because their soul is, like, black, ok). The genre spilled out of post-punk (Siouxsie and the Banshees and The Cure are the bridging acts), but really pivots around Leeds bands Sisters of Mercy and The

Mission. Fans like to think they are vampiric but don't get them confused with *Twilight* fans, as romance has no place in the very serious business of dressing, even on the beach, in black with an ankle-length leather coat and boots like a plaster cast.

ARENA ROCK

Also known as 'stadium rock' or 'corporate rock', this is the natural offspring of 1970s soft rock. The music is designed to get people at the far end of the arena (roughly ten miles from the band) to punch the air wearing those foam 'pointy fingers' you get at baseball games. The Beatles started it by playing Shea Stadium in 1964, but they used speakers the size of shoeboxes and were drowned out by teen screams anyway. Acts like Queen, Kiss, Boston and Journey brought speakers the size of volcanoes and light shows that made Times Square look like a pen torch, and audiences rolled over like stunned donkeys.

COLLEGE ROCK/ALTERNATIVE

The American name for 1980s indie. As the name suggests, it was aimed squarely at college students, as it could be played on local campus radio stations when the major broadcasters wouldn't touch it. That all changed when the poster boys of the scene, R.E.M., signed to major record label Warner and started having hits on 'normal' radio. Bluffers at this point should sigh wistfully and talk about the days when they loved R.E.M. and 10,000 Maniacs before they got successful, lamenting about how 'the corporations' ruined it all. And then, when no one's looking, go for a Starbucks.

INDIE

Music so anaemic and fey it could barely step out in sunlight or climb the stairs without fainting and calling for a bandage and some barley water. It came after post-punk, and the 'indie' was short for the independent labels the music was released on. It shunned success and the charts, instead preferring to grow thick fringes, wear paisley shirts and write love songs based on The Byrds B-sides to girls from the Home Counties dressed in duffel coats. The defining release was the C86 cassette given away free on the cover of indie bible *NME* (*New Musical Express*) in 1986, featuring bands like The Soup Dragons, (very early) Primal Scream and The Mighty Lemon Drops.

INDUSTRIAL

Coming out of punk rock, industrial had much noisier and darker ambitions by pushing rock through experimental and electronic sieves to create a more sinister brew. The name is there to suggest music created by machines in the spirit of heavy industry – a bit like a sheet metal factory trying to do karaoke. Many of the original acts reached a certain cult level (like Swans, Throbbing Gristle, Pere Ubu and Killing Joke), but the superstars of the scene are (to a lesser extent) Ministry and (to a greater extent) Nine Inch Nails.

GRUNGE

A genre synonymous with Seattle in the USA's north-west, and particularly local independent record label, Sub Pop. It was a variation on the doomy heavy metal of Black Sabbath and tied to the 'no sell-out' parochial nature of hardcore punk. Grubby, greasy and dirty, it sounds a bit like a lorry engine screaming about how its parents didn't understand it. The look was lank hair, jeans like Swiss cheese and burst trainers, all topped off with a lumberjack shirt stolen from a bloke eight times your size. Bands like Tad and Mudhoney might have started the scene, but it was Nirvana and Pearl Jam which had the success.

BRITPOP

What used to be called 'indie' in the 1980s – a knock-kneed genre so self-conscious it didn't dare look through its lank fringe at the charts – had become a lot more ambitious by the early 1990s. Disputes over its origins still rage today – was Blur's 'Popscene' or Suede's 'The Drowners' the first Britpop record? Its sound was very much harking back to the 1960s and obsessed with singing about English (not British) things in an English (not British) accent. Other leading lights were Pulp and Elastica, but the big showdown it all led up to was Oasis battling Blur for a number-one single in 1995. By then any idiot in a tracksuit top and vintage trainers singing about eating biscuits in their nan's tower-block flat was getting signed, and the smart ones moved on and it all exploded in self-parody. And cocaine. And heroin.

RAP ROCK/SPORTS METAL

The ugliest-looking and ugliest-sounding sub-genre of rock of all time and, indeed, undisputed owner of the title of the Absolute Worst Music Ever Made by Humans (probably). It took the very worst elements of rap music and rock and shackled them together. Bands (if they can even be called that) like Limp Bizkit – note the appalling spelling, celebrating the nauseating knuckleheadedness of it all – and Blink-182 ran around in hockey tops, baseball caps and voluminous shorts singing songs about getting 'wasted' and hoping to catch a pre-tumescent look at some bare ladies.

EMO

Short for 'emotional', this was somewhere between 1980s indie, goth, glam and a really long letter to an agony aunt about how your parents didn't love you and that girl from your history class broke your heart. Acts like Jimmy Eat World, Dashboard Confessional and Panic! at the Disco had some success in the early 2000s as revivalists of the sound, but it can be tracked back to the 1980s where it was part of the hardcore punk scene and had the ludicrous name of 'emocore' (a truncation of 'emotional hardcore'). Pass the Kleenex.

POST-ROCK

What comes after rock? Post-rock, of course. Has a lot of its DNA in progressive rock and Krautrock (an experimental music form originating in Germany in the late 1960s, synonymous with bands Can, Faust and Neu!), trying very hard to create sprawling pieces of music that are mostly devoid of lyrics and instead use the sounds to intone a creeping sense of doom. Pretentiously using 'rock instruments to make non-rock music', it seemed ashamed of both rock music and fun. The key bands – Bark Psychosis, Tortoise, Mogwai, Godspeed You! Black Emperor – are not just deep and intense, they were deeply deep and intensely intense. If they came to your house for dinner, they wouldn't eat anything and would instead sit on the floor and glare at you until you chased them out with some harmonies and melodies.

MATH ROCK

Believe it or not there really is a genre of music called math rock. What does it sound like? Well, very much like rock music short-circuiting after having to do really difficult long division with 15-figure fractions. What math rock wants to do is tie rhythms, song structures, melodies, time signatures and composition into a giant knot and roll the whole lot at the audience, a bit like in the opening of that Indiana Jones film *Raiders of the Lost Ark*. It is the ultimate test for bluffers because stating that you like it means there is a real chance a math rock fan will make you listen to some new album that sounds like a calculator having a tantrum.

ROCK FASHION AND TRIBES

In over a half-century of rock, numerous tribes have grown and flourished, each trying to distinguish themselves from the styles and traditions of their predecessors.

Bluffers have two options here. Grab a tribe and dress the part for the rest of your life – a serious lifestyle and sartorial commitment – or gain a working knowledge of lots of different tribes and keep wearing your normal clothes while proclaiming yourself aloof and 'not tied to one tribe'. The latter option is probably best, so here's an introduction to who the main tribes are, what they like and, most importantly, how you can spot them based on what they wear.

TEDDY BOYS

These are rock 'n' roll fans inspired to some extent by the dandyism of the Edwardian period. The name morphed into 'Teddy' and Britain's first teen tribal subculture was born. The look was based on drape jackets, drainpipe trousers (worn deliberately short so that socks are exposed), bootlace ties and brothel-creeper shoes. Hair was teased into an improbable quiff and combed into a 'duck's arse' at the back. Teddy boys today look like Morrissey's granddad.

ROCKABILLY

The US side of the Teddy boy coin, rockabilly conjoined the terms 'rock' and 'hillbilly' (meaning US country music) to describe the teens doing bow-legged dances to the new rock 'n' roll of the 1950s. Men dressed in jeans and either denim or leather jackets and looked like an army of Fonz-from-*Happy-Days* clones while the girls got the long straw with polka-dot puffy dresses and bright headscarves. Gingham features heavily, making the overall look *Little House on the Prairie* with quiffs. The later rockabilly style was best exemplified by the 1980s American band Stray Cats, which was much underrated.

MERSEYBEAT

The early 1960s Liverpudlian look was inspired by the Hamburg scene – all leather to start with, and then matching tight-fitting collarless Pierre Cardin suits with waistcoats, white shirts and skinny leather ties. Chelsea boots (aka 'Beatle boots') were, seemingly, compulsory and their high heels left an entire Merseyside generation with corns and fallen arches. And that was just the men.

MODS

The most style-conscious youth group of all time with an emphasis on bespoke suits, and soundtracked by 1960s R&B, beat music, ska and soul. While the music came from the USA, the look and lifestyle was entirely Italian – with coffee bars (then a reasonably new import to the UK) and scooters with more mirrors than Liberace's dressing room. The name derives from 'modernism', an irony that was seemingly lost on the mod revivals of the 1970s (that birthed, among others, The Jam) and the 1990s (that led to Britpop).

Hippies are probably the least hygiene-conscious subculture of all time.

HIPPIES

Probably the least hygiene-conscious subculture of all time, hippies adopted a mantra of 'dropping out' from society. This meant drain-faced, white, middle-class kids with lifeless long hair, dressed in loon pants and ponchos spending all day sprawled across filthy beanbags in a squat beside bongs and bowls of soapy lentils. If they could afford one, they tended to favour evil-smelling 'Afghan coats'. Virgin boss Richard Branson ('the hippie entrepreneur') was said to wear an Afghan in his youth, and is the only hippie in history who ever did a day's work. And he wasn't even a real hippie.

GLAM ROCK

The early 1970s was a grey time for the UK. Fortunately, Marc Bolan changed from cross-legged acoustic elf with Tyrannosaurus Rex to a Technicolor and glitter-doused sex elf in ladies' shoes with T. Rex in 1970 with 'Hot Love'. Hot on his ballet pump heels were David Bowie with *Ziggy Stardust* (glam in space) and Roxy Music (glam and 1940s Hollywood in space), and soon the whole country was in make-up, granny blouses, BacoFoil trousers and platform boots, stomp-dancing to songs about androgyny.

HAIR METAL

The 1970s glam era went off the scale in the LA music scene of the 1980s. While Bon Jovi, Guns N' Roses and Mötley Crüe became hugely successful, the majority of acts were unspeakably average and were judged mainly on the scale of their bleached and backcombed hair (like a hay bale exploding in slow motion) and vertiginous nature of their high heels, rather than their dreary music.

METAL (THRASH)

In stark contrast to the pop sounds and 'disoriented hen night' look of hair metal, 1980s thrash/speed metal was a back-to-basics affair where bands and fans all wore exactly the same clothes, breaking the barrier between the stage and the mosh pit (*see* 'Glossary', page 120).

The look was simple: hair spewing out of the top of their heads like lava, sleeveless black T-shirts (featuring a jagged logo overlaying what looked like a toddler's drawing of a Scooby-Doo monster), black jeans so tight they were probably stitched on in situ, and enormous white basketball boots like two duvets tied in a knot.

PROG ROCK

While prog kingpins Pink Floyd dressed like millionaire hippies (clean jeans and T-shirts), other prog acts went above and beyond the call of duty by dressing like a giant flower (Peter Gabriel of Genesis) or else wrapping themselves in capes and performing shows with King Arthur dancers careering into each other on the UK's ice rinks (Rick Wakeman).

PUNKS (AMERICAN AND BRITISH)

US punk was more based on having no money (see the Ramones' uniform of broken Converse, T-shirts, crumbling jeans and leather jackets), whereas UK punk was more stylised, taking its cue from the fetish gear on sale in Pistols manager Malcolm McLaren's boutique called Sex (bondage trousers, rubber T-shirts, chains) and the spraying of slogans on boiler suits and shirts typified by The Clash. The two looks overlapped (Richard Hell of the Voidoids is the 'virus' that spread on both sides of the Atlantic) and the origins of the style are still pedantically chewed over like chicken wings.

NEW ROMANTICS

As UK punk and new wave either ran out of steam or collapsed into an orgy of burlesque, a new club scene emerged in 1980s London in places like Blitz that abandoned detuned guitars for synths and 'Never Mind The Bollocks' T-shirts for a revisiting of 1970s glam, with David Bowie and Roxy Music being held up like sacrosanct icons. This was compressed into English romanticism, as well as the lost glamour of Hollywood and cabaret, to create a look that was high on 'impact' (heavily painted faces, highly stylised drag). It veered wildly from the Comanche-chic and Highwayman-camp of Adam Ant to the frilly white shirts, thigh-length boots, and baggy pantaloons (with waist-scarf, naturally) of Spandau Ballet.

INDIE KIDS

'Moping' is the best way to describe indie kids during the 1980s and their concerns were mainly about 'The Bomb', fear about finding a sexual partner (and then more fear about what to do if they succeeded), existential poetry and where to get nice duffel coats. Uniforms included Dr Martens boots, Breton shirts, greatcoats and pudding-bowl haircuts or, after The Smiths broke, quiffs and NHS specs. Bluffers need not fear indie kids, as they are, even if you are rumbled, too soft to argue back.

GOTHS

The more death-like one can look, the better. Be careful, though, as just wearing black is not enough in itself, so look out for more telltale signs like studded choker chains, voluminous gowns made from Victorian velvet, hair like a crow flying into a mirror, half-read Mary Shelley hardbacks and a willingness to drink cider by war memorials or graveyards. They're goths.

MADCHESTER

So called because it involved bands from Manchester at the fag end of the 1980s who made 'mad' dance-rock music that was inspired by (illegal drug alert) Ecstasy and acid house music. Happy Mondays and The Stone Roses were the anointed leaders of the scene and the look was 'baggy hooligan' in tops that a Sumo wrestler might send back as 'a bit on the loose side', voluminous flares with each leg having its own postcode, Kickers boots (ideally red but rarely seen as they lay under the flares' denim avalanche) and a bucket hat.

GRUNGE

Had the utilitarian look of truck drivers or loggers – jeans riddled with holes, boots or filthy Converse, plaid shirts – topped off with hair normally seen in a shampoo commercial 'before' shot and T-shirts of bands that no one has ever heard of. After Nirvana broke in 1991, fashion designers tried to co-opt this 'anti-fashion' on the catwalks of Paris while the originators of the look were sleeping on an exposed mattress in a house with every window broken, and a couple of fridges and an upturned sofa in the front yard.

BRITPOP

Combined sharp suits with what Alan Partridge termed 'sports casual' (jeans, retro sports tops, Fred Perry shirts, Dr Martens or Green Flash trainers). While Suede, Blur, Pulp and early Oasis made enduring music that also captured the mood of mid-1990s Britain, the scene quickly collapsed into second- and third-generation copies where bands thought they could 'become Britpop' simply by singing about cups of tea and fried bread in the style of Dick Van Dyke in *Mary Poppins*.

EMO

It's NOT goth, OK? Except it's very, very goth. The look involves lots of black eyeliner, visible piercings and hair obscuring one eye to emphasis how intensely they feel the world. Bluffers should discuss 'emo fakers' with emos and let them ramble on about how they are not emos (they are) but it's not fair how emos are misunderstood. Tip: if they still have a Myspace account, they're emo.

LIVE AND DANGEROUS

Venues are the beating heart of music, the crucibles where new styles are formed and legends are forged in the white heat of ROCK. Bluffers should always express preference for an act's live work over and above their recorded material. At this point, you should mention that no band has ever satisfactorily captured their raw live sound on record and then nod knowingly.

But to put live flesh on the bones of your bluff, you have to be able to discuss the landmark venues, festivals and shows that have really dictated the shape and development of rock. Not all of them are what you (or your audience) might expect. But keeping them guessing lies at the root of all successful bluffing.

VENUES YOU NEED TO KNOW ABOUT

Cavern and Star Clubs

The wellspring for the ever-growing Beatles nostalgia industry, both The Cavern Club (Liverpool) and the

Star-Club (Hamburg) were, as venues, little to write home about, being both cramped and dank. But it's what they represent that matters to rock fans – the totemistic places where The Beatles cut their teeth and earned their chops before the world was looking. At the mention of either, you will allow yourself to sound melancholic and talk about how 'preservation orders' should have been issued for The Cavern (a 'new Cavern' sits a few hundred feet up Mathew Street like a bad TV impressionist) and more health and safety measures applied to the Star-Club (it closed in 1969 and the building that housed it burned down in 1987).

Marquee

You should, if asked about the Marquee, respond by asking which Marquee. There were three major sites and then two subsequent sites because some buffoon in a marketing agency thought the 'brand' could be replicated in inadequate venues. The original Marquee stood on Oxford Street in London and was primarily a jazz venue, but rock bluffers get points for mentioning that The Rolling Stones first played there in 1962. By 1964 it had moved round the corner to Wardour Street and that's where the legend really grew. The Who, Led Zeppelin, Jimi Hendrix and Pink Floyd all played there in the 1960s, while by the late 1970s it had also helped give painful birth to punk. In the 1980s it was known as a metal venue and in 1988 the venue was relocated to Charing Cross Road on the other side of Soho and that – despite a 2001 move to open it again in Islington and a doomed attempt in 2003/2004 to place it in Leicester Square – was the end of that.

100 Club

Standing at, as the name suggests, number 100 Oxford Street in London, it has, like the Marquee, a diverse and almost schizophrenic history. So you'll need to think strategically about what era of the club's life you want to pass yourself off as an expert on. Opening in 1942, the basement venue was a jazz club, but by 1976 a whole new generation had taken over. Many London venues claim to have been where punk was born but the 100 Club can perhaps claim the greatest impact for hosting the first 'international punk festival' (September 1976), featuring many of the scene's leading acts and where a girl in the audience lost an eye after a glass, allegedly thrown by Sid Vicious, shattered off a pillar and hit her in the face. Dear old Sid; he always got the blame.

CBGB

To gain extra kudos, you should refer to it under its full name of CBGB OMFUG (Country, Bluegrass and Blues and Other Music For Uplifting Gormandizers). This dive in the Bowery in Manhattan was the ultimate 'toilet venue' as the urinals would often block and spill out into the club. This, you should note, made it 'real' and not simply a health hazard. It opened in 1973 but, after the closure of the Mercer Arts Center where the New York Dolls held court, it soon became the place where the city's nascent punk bands – Suicide, Television and Patti Smith notably – would play. Then a whole scene, in which the Ramones and Blondie had the most success, coalesced into what was basically an open sewer with beer on tap. It closed in 2006 and a fashion boutique, created by menswear designer John Varvatos, replaced it. The jeans it sells are not disintegrating like those the Ramones wore – and will set you back several hundred dollars a pair.

Troubadour

Founded in 1957, this venue in West Hollywood effectively invented the FM sound of the 1970s. Initially a folk venue, it became the launch pad for many of the biggest confessional singer-songwriter acts of the 1970s – Joni Mitchell, Carole King, Jackson Browne, James Taylor, Carly Simon – as well as the place where Elton John played his first US show. If the Troubadour had never opened, it's likely that long periods of the 1970s would have happened in total silence.

The Fillmore

San Francisco's answer to the Troubadour in the 1960s, it struck pay dirt in 1967's Summer of Love as it showcased most of the city's psychedelic acts – including Jefferson Airplane and Quicksilver Messenger Service – as well as others like Hendrix and The Doors, on top of hosting gigs by Miles Davis, Otis Redding and Aretha Franklin. All of that should, in theory, make this the coolest venue in rock history. You should, however, be aware that the venue was key to the career of the Grateful Dead and, as such, should have been closed down immediately for immeasurable crimes against music. In any discussion about The Fillmore, you should also recall that famous quote, attributed to Grace Slick: 'If you remember the 60s, you weren't really there.'

Whisky A Go Go

As long as there has been a rock scene in Los Angeles, Whisky A Go Go has been the place to see and be seen. Located on the Sunset Strip, it has all the credentials to be considered perhaps the coolest and most decadent venue that ever put a band on. It is, in club terms, the equivalent of Iggy Pop, Lemmy, Keith Richards and Ozzy Osbourne all living together in a house made out of empty Jack Daniel's bottles. Bluffers will know the first Whisky venue was in Chicago (opening in 1958) and the LA one opened in 1964, effectively making it a chain venue akin to today's Waxy O'Connor's Irish bars. The Doors were, for a short period, the house band but got sacked for playing incest-themed 'The End'.

FESTIVALS YOU NEED TO KNOW ABOUT

Monterey

The prototype for the modern festival happened in Monterey in California in June 1967, the Summer of Love (which of course, you won't remember because you were there; *see* above). Acts included The Who, The Jimi Hendrix Experience, Janis Joplin, Jefferson Airplane and Otis Redding. It is probably more famous for the acts they tried to get but who, for whatever reason, decided to stay at home and have access to their own toilets rather than a gurgling bubbling trench. They included The Beatles, Captain Beefheart, The Kinks, half the Motown roster and (because someone forgot to invite them) The Doors. Monterey was the inspiration for every major rock festival that has ever followed. The organisers learned quickly. Never again was Ravi Shankar allowed to play the sitar all afternoon.

Woodstock

The birth of the super-festival happened in Woodstock (in upstate New York) over 'three days of peace and music' in August 1969. The place was, and let's not hold back here, overrun with hippies with even less access to showers than normal and the site was rocked by rain, dramatic overcrowding (conservative estimates say half a million people were there) and dangers wrought by the infamous and widely available 'brown acid', a substance so noxious that legendary DJ Wavy Gravy had to make an announcement on stage that there was some bad stuff going around giving people seriously negative vibes, man. It continued to rain, a lot. The hippies even tried to 'think' the rain to stop. Joni Mitchell had the right idea, writing a song about it (called, amazingly, 'Woodstock') but not actually attending. They tried to revive it several times – most notoriously in 1999 when they got awful bands like Limp Bizkit to play. The audience rioted and burned down the toilets – an achingly poignant tribute. An attempt to hold a 50th anniversary version in August 2019 ran into all manner of problems and was cancelled. If asked to point to the most memorable moment of the 1969 festival, say that it was unquestionably Hendrix's imperious rendition of 'The Star-Spangled Banner'.

Glastonbury also has alarmingly high numbers of hippies on the site – even in these days of affordable antibacterial wet wipes.

Glastonbury

Somerset's rolling version of Woodstock also has alarmingly high numbers of hippies on the site – even in these days of affordable (and biodegradable) antibacterial wet wipes. It started in 1970 and usually takes place on the weekend of June closest to summer solstice in the shadow of Glastonbury Tor where several ley lines meet, all of which are like catnip to hippies. Founder Michael Eavis hosts it on his own farm when, for a week most summers, the fields are invaded by refugees from the sprawling conurbations who want to commune with nature and eat an ostrich burger in nine feet of oozing mud while Coldplay (it's always Coldplay) headline the Pyramid stage. The bluffer's tactic might be to opine that the festival lost its spirit when they started televising it and when they put up the 'super-fence' to keep freeloaders and ne'er-do-wells out. Also, you won't much approve of the growing prevalence of 'glamping', and will have stern words to say about staying in a luxury 'yurt' or ecolodge.

Coachella

Or Coachella Valley Music & Arts Festival to give it its full name. It started in 1999 and takes place at the Empire Polo Club in Indio, California. It has frequently been called 'the American Glastonbury' but, frankly, is nothing of the sort. It takes place over two consecutive weekends in April (depending on pandemics) each year where effectively the same acts play twice. It is heavy on the brand presence (a commercial reality for all festivals these days) but perhaps encourages this too much and has become a festival to be seen at rather than one to get lost in the music at. Coachella has an encouragingly diverse line-up but it is so intricately linked with carefully staged social media 'boast posts' that it has been commonly derided as a poseurs' convention and one yawning Instagram 'opportunity'.

GIGS YOU NEED TO KNOW ABOUT

The Beatles play Shea Stadium and the rooftop of Savile Row

Perhaps the two most famous gigs by a band that effectively stopped touring in 1966. Both shows, one enormous and the other tiny, had one thing in common – no one could hear them play. The band's show at Shea Stadium in New York in August 1965 saw The Beatles play to over 55,000 fans who were screaming their tonsils out as the band tried to perform through speakers the size of cereal boxes (the variety pack ones) and puny amps. The band's final show (January 1969) was on the roof of Apple Studios on Savile Row in central London where they accidentally invented the 'guerilla gig'. It was to prove their final gig, not because it went badly, but because they all hated each other by that stage.

Velvet Underground play
the Exploding Plastic Inevitable

The bluffer needs a long run-up to this one, as attendance at these events was low and hardly any footage of the band playing exists. But it is the gig (or, rather, series of gigs) to show knowledge of and express chest-swelling admiration for – simply because the mythology around them is so potent. The Velvet Underground would occasionally play amid oil-wheel projections and showings of Andy Warhol's latest films (this, you should say, made it one of the earliest 'multimedia art happenings').

Dylan goes electric (Newport and Manchester)

In the constant retelling of the story of former folk protest singer Bob Dylan 'going electric', it's become mythologised as being akin to Dylan going over the top and single-handedly winning the First World War. And the Second. And possibly Vietnam. In reality, he showed up at the Newport festival (that had helped launch him in acoustic mode) in 1965, played an acoustic set, then 'plugged in' for two or three songs with a full band and then humbly played 'It's All Over Now, Baby Blue' as an acoustic encore. The irate folkies weren't really that irate, maybe just a bit miffed. Where the legend went several different shapes of wonky was at his 1966 show in the Free Trade Hall in Manchester where second-year undergraduate and irked folk fan Keith Butler heckled him as 'Judas!' before he played his final song, and Dylan responded weakly: 'I don't believe you.'

Butler instantly became the most famous heckler in the world, and was the subject of a number of obituaries when he died in Canada in 2002, aged 56. This is the sort of stuff bluffers should drop casually into conversation.

Altamont

Often referred to in terms of being 'the death of the 1960s dream' by the kind of people who like to understand history in terms of decades that are 'bookended' by 'pivotal moments'. The Rolling Stones decided to have a free festival in December 1969 at the Altamont Speedway in northern California. Except somehow the Hell's Angels took charge of on-site security and an 18-year-old man, Meredith Hunter, got into an altercation and was stabbed to death by one of them. This has taken on great symbolism for the people who like to think the Stones were a dark force to be reckoned with, rather than five ugly blokes from England in their nans' blouses.

Sex Pistols at Lesser Free Trade Hall in Manchester

While London had all the famous venues, you should know that the most symbolic gig during UK punk was when the Sex Pistols were invited by the freshly minted Buzzcocks to play a show in the North in June 1976 that hardly anyone went to. But those that did included future members of Joy Division, The Fall, The Smiths and Factory Records founder Tony Wilson. Oh, and Mick Hucknall from Simply Red. Really.

Live Aid

Not the first charity concert (George Harrison's Concert For Bangladesh predates it by 14 years), but Live Aid was the biggest. It took place in two cities in July 1985 (Wembley Stadium in London and John F. Kennedy Stadium in Philadelphia, with other performances beamed in from places such as Russia and Australia) where just about every major act got a few songs each to raise money for the famine in Ethiopia. You'll need to know two main things about this: 1) Did it revitalise the careers of a load of rock dinosaurs and end up indirectly giving them a windfall when the purpose was to save people from starvation? (Answer: yes.) 2) Who 'won' Live Aid by playing the best set? (Answer: despite every attempt to grab the headlines and camera lenses, Bono and U2 didn't 'win' Live Aid – Queen did.)

Spike Island

Acid house created the second Summer of Love in 1989, but The Stone Roses took a year to organise their version of Woodstock or Monterey. However, they decided to hold the event in a reclaimed toxic waste site in Widnes in the north of England. Those who were there (27,000 tickets were sold but at least 300 times this number claim they were there) will assert it was 'the gig of a generation'; but look into their eyes and see the truth like all good bluffers can. The reality was that the people were stuck there all day, the beer quickly ran out, burgers cost more than a car and when the band came on, the crosswinds meant the sound was carried away from the crowd.

Oasis play Knebworth

Just as Oasis borrowed their look, attitude and swagger from The Stone Roses, so too did they have to borrow the idea of doing their own festival. Led Zeppelin and Queen had previously played the Hertfordshire estate in the 1970s but, this being the Britpop 1990s when the entire music business lost control of its senses (clue: cocaine), everything had to be BIGGER and LOUDER and EVEN BIGGER STILL. So Oasis booked in for two nights in August 1996 to play in front of 300,000 people. Apparently up to 3 million people applied for tickets. While Oasis songwriter Noel Gallagher made lofty pronouncements about its importance ('Has God played Knebworth recently?'), his nose was well and truly put out of joint when Robbie Williams (who Gallagher had termed 'the fat dancer from Take That') played there in 2003 over three nights to crowds of 375,000.

MEDIA MILESTONES

Every bluffer needs at least a fighting chance if caught in a discussion about rock books or films. The list that follows should cover most bases if you're invited to join the discussion. A little knowledge, the saying goes, is a dangerous thing. A lot of knowledge is a boring thing. So the best idea is to take the path of least resistance.

ROCK BOOKS TO KNOW ABOUT

Hammer Of The Gods

Written by Stephen Davis, this is the ultimate tale of rock 'n' roll excess on the road, based on two weeks he spent touring the USA with Led Zeppelin in 1975. The book positively reeks of booze, drugs, the occult and the sort of sexual excesses that would cause the Marquis de Sade to recoil in alarm.

Key moment The fish (some say a red snapper, others a mud shark) being inserted into various parts of a Seattle groupie.

You Never Give Me Your Money

Peter Doggett tries to untangle the complex financial dealings of The Beatles after they split, while simultaneously recounting their story. Despite being a 'business book', the band members come across as greedy, grasping, double-crossing megalomaniacs who were bitterly lassoed together and who ran their finances with all the care of a tornado tearing through a landfill site.

Key moment Representatives scouting out the possibility of a reunion show in New York's Central Park mere weeks before John Lennon is murdered.

Life

Keith Richards has rattled through life since the mid-1960s like a freewheeling drug sponge and yet his autobiography is surprisingly lucid and rich in detail, coming, as it does, from a man who has spent half a century hovering a few feet off the ground like a crumpled crisp packet over an air vent. The tours, the rivalry with Mick Jagger, the women and the drugs – the endless drugs – are spat out with studied nonchalance.

Key moment The dismissal, once and for all, of the Marianne Faithfull/Mars Bar 'story' that long ago passed into urban myth.

Chronicles

Bob Dylan has spent his entire career creating myths about his life (like being an orphan and working the railroads/carnivals) and sending fans off on wild goose chases with every knotted lyric. So it's a hell of a shock to see the first edition of his autobiography shedding powerful light on to whole eras of his life. It's written in sections and has no clear chronology, but at least it's readable, unlike his first book, *Tarantula,* an incredibly tedious and incoherent experimental prose poetry collection that defies further description.

Key moment The evocation of arriving in a freezing New York in 1961, dizzy with promise, as he cracks his knuckles and prepares to turn the world on its head.

Diary Of A Rock 'n' Roll Star

Unlike those books endlessly banging on about excess, Mott The Hoople singer Ian Hunter lays bare just how mundane the whole thing is – a rock purgatory that is only punctured briefly when bands get on stage. Reading this, you don't begrudge bands their on-the-road fun if the rest of the time is really as grindingly dull as Hunter suggests.

Key moment David Bowie (who wrote 'All the Young Dudes' for the band) makes cameo appearances and the pages, so grey with routine, finally crackle.

The Dirt

Mötley Crüe were, and let's not mince our words here, a truly awful band. But their reputation was fished out of the musical gutter with the publication of this four-way group autobiography where each member got to tell their side of what went on. Features enormous hair, horrible guitar solos and a wardrobe based on a Hollywood depiction of what 'streetwalkers' wore in the 1980s. It was turned into a Netflix biopic in 2019.

Key moment Mick Mars falls off his chair in the studio when trying to play the guitar line to 'Girls, Girls, Girls'.

Please Kill Me

An oral history account of New York punk (a publishing template that many have since copied but not as well) by Legs McNeil and Gillian McCain that covers just about everyone in the scene – from band members, venue owners and fanzine writers to fans. The good thing is that bluffers can just pick a few random sections to loosely quote and it will seem like they've read the whole thing.

Key moment Lou Reed meets the Ramones for the first time and tells Johnny to use a better guitar than the $50 one he has, causing Johnny to sulk.

England's Dreaming

Jon Savage's definitive account of UK punk that spends as much time talking about the scene leaders (Sex Pistols and The Clash) as it does about the lesser-known bands (The Slits, X-Ray Spex), and wraps the whole thing up in an intellectual bubble where fanzines are the direct descendants of the pamphleteer movement and Johnny Rotten is merely the latest in a long and healthy line of dissenters in British history who have wanted to destroy the status quo (not Status Quo).

Key moment The Sex Pistols' infamy overtakes them, they become targets for physical assault and so go to ground, robbing the scene of its figureheads.

Never A Dull Moment

Written by journalist and broadcaster David Hepworth, this is less a book and more a thrusting thesis that rock music 'peaked' as an artistic form in 1971. Hepworth uses the key acts and albums of the year (Carole King, Rod Stewart, Rolling Stones, David Bowie and more) to argue his case that rock reached its unrepeatable apotheosis that year. Some may agree that he nails it while others will feel that any compression of a single year into a handful of records selectively elevates the sparse handful of wheat over the cubic hectares of chaff.

Key moment Carole King's majestic *Tapestry* creates a new type of blockbuster album where men (as creators and audience) play second fiddle.

The Year The Decade Exploded

Hepworth might claim 1971, but music writer Jon Savage (yes, him again) argues 1966 is the most important year for music. It is an exhaustive month-by-month analysis of the year that makes a convincing case that it was moving at breakneck speed and it is only at the distance of half a century that we can truly make sense of it all. Rather than just focus on the biggest sellers and the most famous names (although there is plenty of that), Savage also hunts among the weeds to find the records, the books, the artists, the ideas, the politics and the magazines that may have happened at the periphery but that laid the foundations for what we understand today to be popular culture.

Key moment So many to choose from but setting up the compelling argument that Norma Tanega's 'Walkin' My Cat Named Dog' was much, much more than a novelty hit and why she marked the arrival of 'a different kind of female pop star'.

Shock & Awe: Glam Rock & Its Legacy

A proper doorstopper of a book from Simon Reynolds that tells the long history of glam, dressing it gently in the gauze and feathers of the semi-academic peacock. Using Marc Bolan, David Bowie, Lou Reed, Iggy Pop and Alice Cooper as the connective tissue, this is not just revenge on the Sixties by the aforementioned stars who made the Seventies their own, it is also about queer politics melding with a keening 1950s nostalgia, with high-brow and low-brow reference points all crashing in on top of each other to make a glorious mess.

Key moment Making the case for *The Rocky Horror Picture Show* as one of the most important productions (aesthetically and politically) of the 1970s that has perhaps been forgotten in subsequent decades.

ROCK DOCUMENTARIES TO KNOW ABOUT

Don't Look Back/Eat The Document

D.A. Pennebaker followed Bob Dylan on his 1965 UK acoustic tour (*Don't Look Back*) and the following year's electric tour (*Eat the Document*). The former details Dylan upsetting fans and acolytes alike with his studied disdain. The latter was shown once on TV after years of painful re-edits and, because it is in colour, should be referred to by bluffers as the filmic Holy Grail for Dylan nuts.

Key scene Dylan and John Lennon, both enormously refreshed (according to Lennon's own account on 'junk'), sit in the back of a limo for half an hour trying, and failing, to hold it together.

The Beatles Anthology

Only a mammoth undertaking could hope to even tell part of the story of The Beatles that has now become not just the story of the 1960s but also the story of the second half of the twentieth century. Over ten hours, the rise and fall of The Beatles is recounted in exhaustive detail – every sigh, burp and uneaten piece of toast catalogued and analysed. All of The Beatles (except Lennon, who speaks through ghostly archive interviews) are on hand to jolly up what great mates they really were and brush over the fact that they couldn't stand the sight of each other for years.

Key scene The recording of 'Tomorrow Never Knows', the song that sent the band into a whole new world of weirdness.

Dig!

A modern morality tale told from the perspective of two bands – The Dandy Warhols (who had some success) and Brian Jonestown Massacre (who sabotaged every part of their careers like Wile E. Coyote on bad drugs). The Warhols were, let's say, heavily influenced by the Jonestowns but got the big record deal and hit singles while Anton Newcombe's Jonestowns couldn't hold on to members, stay out of trouble with the law or avoid upsetting everyone in the music industry who could possibly help them. They thought the way to play a gig was to kick audience members in the face.

Key scene After an on-stage scuffle, Anton sulks outside the venue before screaming at the band member he blames for the wreckage, 'You f***ing broke my sitar, mother****er!'

Cocksucker Blues

Never formally released, the film follows The Rolling Stones on their 1972 tour of the USA to promote *Exile on Main St* and is shot *cinéma-vérité* style – which is a posh way of saying cameras were everywhere and caught everything (mostly erratically) on film. Think of the worst thing a band can do on the road. Rest assured that it's on there and it's one of the tamer scenes. The band, especially 'Sir' Mick Jagger, have tried to keep a lid on the film but bootleg copies ensure it remains out there and has become the central text for their bacchanalia.

Key scene Keith Richards' heroin addiction is reaching a crescendo while, ironically, the man himself spends a lot of time just nodding off.

Keith Richards' heroin addiction is reaching a crescendo while, ironically, the man himself spends a lot of time just nodding off.

The Last Waltz

Martin Scorsese films the last show by The Band (in San Francisco's Winterland Ballroom) in November 1976. Despite the fact that a cocaine tsunami had engulfed everyone within a three-mile radius of the venue, it is commonly hailed as the greatest concert film of all time. Scorsese's filming is a joy and the whole show features guest appearances from serious stars like Muddy Waters,

Joni Mitchell, Bob Dylan, Neil Diamond, Eric Clapton and, most hilariously of all, Van Morrison – sweating in a sparkly purple suit and looking like a garden gnome at a wedding.

Key scene Footage of Neil Young had to be retouched in the edit to cover up a suspicious fist-sized ball of caked white powder dangling from his nostril. Young has since admitted that he was using cocaine regularly around this time. Look carefully and you can still see some shadowy remnants of the snow bogey in the doctored edit.

The Great Rock 'n' Roll Swindle

Sex Pistols manager Malcolm McLaren (calling himself The Embezzler) tries to simultaneously build and destroy the myth of the Sex Pistols, presenting his film as a step-by-step guide to how he made the most notorious band in the country bend to his will. It features a narrative device whereby Pistols guitarist Steve Jones is a private detective trying to unpick what happened with the band and why Johnny Rotten walked out. A last gasp for the band and a memorable exercise in shameless bluffing by McLaren that should be an object lesson for everyone who reads this book.

Key scene Sid Vicious steals a huge slice of strawberry flan and then tries to scrawl his name on the overalls of a Parisienne who works in the cake shop. Poor old Sid.

Some Kind Of Monster

A 2004 documentary on heavy metal's most dysfunctional multimillionaires, Metallica. The band have an album (*St Anger*) to record, except they can't bear to be in the same room with each other, bass player Jason Newsted has quit and singer James Hetfield is bound for rehab. The band becomes ever reliant on a group counsellor (Phil Towle) to get them all vaguely heading in the same direction. Every scene burns with earnest desperation.

Key scene Drummer Lars Ulrich says to Hetfield (who's wearing dungarees), 'You're just sitting there being a complete dick!', as guitarist Kirk Hammett is seen smacking his forehead in exasperation.

The Decline Of Western Civilization Part II: The Metal Years

Penelope Spheeris witnesses the comi-tragedy that fuels the 1980s heavy metal scene in a documentary that will make you squirm like a bag of snakes. An unsteady Ozzy Osbourne shows up trying to make breakfast (he pours orange juice everywhere), while the lazy misogyny of many performers is used like a never-ending noose with which to hang them, notably Kiss frontman Paul Stanley, looking like someone's unwanted uncle, sprawling on a bed with groupies as he modestly explains how irresistible people find him.

Key scene Chris Holmes, lead guitarist of W.A.S.P., in an inflatable chair pouring vodka over his head as his own mother sighs in resignation.

Meeting People Is Easy

Millionaire megastars Radiohead make a documentary

about how unspeakably awful it is to be successful and venerated. The charitable view is that they intended to show the flipside to being a successful band – namely the constant travel, the dislocation, the engulfing ennui, being burned out, and all those other things they sing about. In reality, it looks like pampered pop stars having a self-indulgent moan about a lifestyle most of us wouldn't mind enjoying for a year or two, or 70.

Key scene Singer Thom Yorke tries to go incognito in the street but gets hassled for being the guy who wrote 'Creep'.

loudQUIETloud

In 2004, Pixies reunited for a highly successful run of shows. They were never a band to 'communicate' among each other so it was a risky endeavour to have a documentary crew follow them around in such a high-pressure situation. It is awkward to begin with, then they get on but inevitably old animosities – in part triggered by addiction issues and family problems – bubble back up to the surface during what should have been their lap of honour. At times it is touching and at times really difficult to watch – but it does expose just how fragile inter-band relations are. You are left with the conclusion that it is a miracle that these people could collectively have made the incredible music they did.

Key scene Drummer David Lovering doing magic tricks on stage every night as the opening act for his own band.

MAGAZINES

Crawdaddy!

A title to sort the real bluffers from the semi-bluffers, the late American music journalist Paul Williams created it in 1966. As the self-styled first US magazine of rock 'n' roll criticism, it regarded itself as 'the first magazine to take rock and roll seriously'.

Rolling Stone

Rock writing goes mainstream in the 1960s when Jann Wenner founds the title in 1967, aged 21. The fact that he is still publisher more than half a century later has led to accusations that it is rather stuck in the past.

NME

Founded in 1952, it was also the first to publish the UK charts later that year (based on publisher Maurice Kinn ringing a handful of record shops and asking what was selling). Each generation has its favourite period of the paper (such as the 'hip young gunslingers' era of the ill-matched, briefly married Julie Burchill and Tony Parsons, the faux-intellectual 1980s, the Madchester-to-Britpop years, etc.). No matter what era you are tied to, the default position is to say 'it's not as good as it was', despite the fact that 1) it is still as good as it was; and 2) the people who say that haven't seen it for 20 years. In sharp decline since the early 2000s, it became a free sheet in 2015, but that was just delaying the inevitable. It published its last print edition in March 2018 but the nme.com site marches on.

Q

Originally intended to be called *Cue* until someone pointed out that it might be mistaken for a snooker magazine, it completely changed the music magazine world when it arrived in the mid-1980s. It was monthly, full colour and glossy (the main weekly music papers were called 'inkies' as the ink came off on your hands), and was in possession of a sense of humour and an arched eyebrow – simultaneously celebrating the amazingness and utter ridiculousness of rock.

Mojo

Designed as the classic rock magazine that *Q* readers 'grew into', *Mojo* is owned by the same publisher and takes a longer and more serious look at the history of music, although it will occasionally write about new acts (which are unlikely to make the cover). It's a good place for bluffers to quickly glean scraps of information about major heritage rock acts as well as those living in the more obscure nooks. One issue will give you bluffing fuel for months.

The Word

A relatively short-lived magazine (2003–2012), it lived up to its taglines of 'At last – something to read!' and 'Entertainment for lively minds' by covering not just rock music but also the worlds linked to it (TV, cinema, books) and the world that shrouded it (the music business). It had a respected podcast series but it was its online readership community (aka The Massive) that really showed how magazines in the digital age could still matter to people.

Many rock stars pile up in the Great Rock Scrapyard when their Faustian debt is called in. These, you can state solemnly, are the ones who fall foul of the dangers of rock.

DANGER! ROCKS

Rock music, or more specifically the lifestyle associated with rock music, is one fraught with immense danger. Admittedly, much of it is the creation of rock stars themselves when fame, money and whatever else they can get their hands on creates a perfect storm of hedonism.

Many, fortunately, make it out the other end relatively unscathed. Many others, however, are less fortunate and pile up in the Great Rock Scrapyard when their Faustian debt is called in. These, you can state solemnly, are the ones who fall foul of the dangers of rock.

THE 27 CLUB

It is thus called because in order to gain membership, all you have to do is be a famous rock star and die at the age of 27. Much has been made of the 'live fast, die young, leave a good-looking corpse' mythology, but it all seems a great waste to have, at best, a few years of success only to have it all snuffed out just to conform to an audience's vicarious sense of what a rock star is 'supposed' to do. Members of this auspicious club include Robert Johnson, Brian Jones, Jimi Hendrix, Janis Joplin, Jim Morrison, Chris Bell (of Big Star), Kurt Cobain and Amy Winehouse. Cobain's mother summed it up perfectly – all that pointless abandon and wasted talent – when she called it 'that stupid club'.

… In order to gain membership, all you have to do is be a famous rock star and die at the age of 27. Much has been made of the 'live fast, die young, leave a good-looking corpse' mythology, but it all seems a great waste …

GETTING THE BOOT AS FAME AND FORTUNE BECKON

Spare a thought for those band members who went through all the pain and misery of trying to make it, only to 'collect their cards' the moment The Big Time comes knocking. Many bands have a period of mixing and matching to find the perfect line-up, but top of the bill for getting turned away when within tantalising touching distance of the velvet rope is Pete Best. He joined The Beatles in 1960 and went through the Hamburg years but was laid off in August 1962 and replaced by Ringo Starr. In February 1963 the band were at number 1 in the singles chart with 'Please Please Me'. That, frankly, has got to hurt.

GETTING YOUR COLLAR FELT

Most rock stars like to present themselves as outlaws. In reality, they have access to the best lawyers in the world and so can afford to be relatively untouchable. Some, however, do stumble a little and serve time in the Big House, almost always for possession of drugs. Mick Jagger and Keith Richards both were busted in the 1960s and even cuddly Sir Paul McCartney has been arrested multiple times for possession of 'fab gear' (cannabis, the growing of which was once defended on the grounds of his 'keen interest in horticulture'), and you'd be forgiven for thinking former Libertines co-frontman Pete Doherty seemingly gets arrested more often than most people buy a newspaper. There are less 'acceptable' reasons for them to go to chokey such as murder (Phil Spector) and abuse of minors (Gary Glitter). Oh dear.

BEING ACCUSED OF PUTTING HIDDEN MESSAGES IN YOUR MUSIC

This is ripe territory for bluffing, and you can safely make up as many outlandish claims as you want. If the message is hidden or subliminal, who can possibly dispute its existence? Bands accused of this nefarious practice include Led Zeppelin (satanism in 'Stairway to Heaven'), The Beatles ('covering up' the 'death' of

Paul McCartney in both 'I'm So Tired' and 'Revolution Number 9'), smoking drugs (Queen in 'Another One Bites The Dust') and encouraging fans to kill themselves ('Better by You, Better Than Me' by Judas Priest). It is all, of course, total tosh but some acts incorporate such messages to muck about with the woolly heads of impressionable listeners with nothing better to do than play LPs backwards and 'decode' them. The practice of recording backwards is sometimes known as 'backmasking', and is apparently popular with those who have a 'satanic' message. And while we're on the subject …

BEING ACCUSED OF BEING IN LEAGUE WITH THE DEVIL

It all started with the mythology around Robert Johnson, but many acts have also been accused of being in league with the devil – such as The Rolling Stones (admittedly not helped by the fact they had a song called 'Sympathy for the Devil'), Kiss (their name, one nutter asserted, was an acronym for 'Kids in Satan's Service'), Led Zeppelin (because of guitarist Jimmy Page's 'keen' interest in the work of occultist Aleister Crowley) and pretty much everyone involved in heavy metal (although some of them really are satanists). Most bands like to play around with the symbolism, as it looks like they are dangerously dabbling with the dark side, but in reality they probably have to sleep with the light on.

The music business has been compared
to a log flume of cocaine with
rolled up £50 notes instead of logs.

SUICIDE/DISAPPEARANCE

The real dark side of rock is not satanism, but rather the inability for some to handle the fame, temptations and pressures weighing heavily on their relatively young shoulders. Some opt out by simply cutting themselves off from the music industry (like early Pink Floyd frontman Syd Barrett and Fleetwood Mac's Peter Green) but tragically others choose to end it themselves (Kurt Cobain, Joy Division singer Ian Curtis) or else disappear completely (Richey Edwards of Manic Street Preachers).

DRUGS AND MELTDOWNS

The music business has been compared to a log flume of cocaine with rolled up £50 notes instead of logs. Many rock stars dabble for a year or two and then write songs or give interviews to *Hello!* about how they got 'clean' before going off to live on a diet of organic seeds, wheatgrass and alfalfa up a mountain somewhere. Others, however, are not so lucky and are sent spiralling into a tailspin they never quite pull out of. You will know that two of the most prominent casualties are Syd Barrett (ibid.), once famously performing with a potion of crushed Mandrax tranquilliser tablets and Brylcreem smeared over his head, and Brian Wilson, retreating to a piano in a sandbox as he became increasingly unable to cope with the outside world.

SEX TAPES

When fame arrives, unattractive 'stars' of both sexes gorge on sex like starving animals. With yawning inevitability, this leads to the 'sex tape' that is made and then somehow leaked online, usually around the same time that the rock star's fame is taking a nosedive. Those who have ended up 'showing it all' include Tommy Lee, Vince Neil and, most terrifying of all, Fred Durst of Limp Bizkit. Fortunately there isn't yet a group video of the Butthole Surfers and Throbbing Gristle in a naked sex romp (as far as we know).

BEING MURDERED

Fame does funny things to people and triggers unpredictably emotional responses among both those who are famous and people living in the shadow of fame. John Lennon was gunned down outside his New York home by Mark Chapman in 1980, Marvin Gaye was shot dead by his own father in 1984, and the drowning of ex-Rolling Stone Brian Jones in 1969 has long been suspected to be the result of very dark dealings. It's even more common in hip-hop (Tupac, Notorious BIG, etc.) which, in comparison, makes rock seem like the kind of place where everyone gets a carriage clock for long service.

DYING ON THE ROAD

'The day the music died', memorably referenced in Don McLean's 'American Pie', was 3 February 1959 when a plane carrying Buddy Holly, Ritchie Valens and The Big Bopper crashed shortly after taking off from Clear Lake, Iowa. None of them survived. Half of Lynyrd Skynyrd were wiped out in a plane crash in Gillsburg, Mississippi, while Ozzy Osbourne's guitarist Randy Rhoads went to the great gig in the sky when a prank to 'buzz' the band's tour bus in a small plane went horribly wrong. Both Eddie Cochran (April 1960) and T. Rex's Marc Bolan (September 1977) met their maker after a car crash. There are others. Being 'on the road' is not a safe place for rock stars. Or any of the rest of us come to that.

CHOKING ON VOMIT

In the 'mockumentary' *This Is Spinal Tap*, the band reminisce about the long line of their drummers who passed away in mysterious circumstances. Eric 'Stumpy Joe' Childs, we find out, bowed out after choking on vomit – someone else's vomit ('You can't really dust for vomit,' points out guitarist Nigel Tufnel about the forensic dead end). Vomit-choking is one of the biggest 'silent' killers in rock, with AC/DC's first singer Bon Scott, original Stereophonics drummer Stuart Cable, Led Zeppelin's John Bonham, and the great Jimi Hendrix all exiting this way. There are definitely more dignified ways to go.

BEING BANNED

Ban them and then no one will hear their dreadful messages! Except for people who had never heard of those messages in the first place, and who will definitely not want to find out what everyone is up in arms about. The fractured logic of the Parents' Music Resource Center in the 1980s saw them put enormous 'parental advisory' stickers on albums warning of their dangerous content. They thought it would kill album sales and careers. In fact, it boosted both, and having a PMRC sticker on your album was something bands actually aspired towards earning. The PMRC could well have been a brilliantly conceived rock industry marketing initiative.

Female rock stars tend not to be quite so susceptible to maternity suits. The defence of 'How do I know it's mine?' rarely holds water.

CAUSING RIOTS

Some bands saw creating a riot of some sort as an intrinsic part of the show (early Jesus and Mary Chain concerts ended, boringly and inevitably, with a riot) while others happened simply because the acts didn't think about what they were doing, couldn't play properly, insulted their audience, stormed off or even failed to show up. Guns N' Roses are no stranger to this sort of behaviour, but by the time it starts kicking off and the seats start to arc through the air, the bands are in limos speeding into the night, miles from the venue. If they ever got near there in the first place.

DIVORCE/PATERNITY SUITS

Some rock stars' partners turn a blind eye to promiscuity (in a 'what happens on tour stays on tour' process of denial), but others are less forgiving and so the whole grubby car crash of the relationship is dragged through the divorce courts, much to the delight of the gutter press. Prenuptial agreements are a relatively recent proactive step to make the inevitable fallout less expensive, but they can only alleviate the financial sting so much when children are involved. Then, of course, there's the constant anxiety of being frog-marched off to a paternity test nine months after playing in a small town in the middle of nowhere. Loneliness and boredom on the road is difficult to deal with, and one thing can lead to another. Sometimes, paternity can be called into question many years later – a constant source of anxiety for old rockers. Female rock stars tend not to be quite so susceptible to maternity suits. The defence of 'How do I know it's mine?' rarely holds water.

OVEREATING AND 'COKE BLOAT'

Rock stars are praised for their whippet-like appearance, razor-sharp hip bones/cheek bones and a waist like a thimble. It's a sign of the 'wasted' and 'decadent' lifestyle – they're too busy rocking to eat a decent meal. For years that works, but then their metabolism slows down and, as they tour less frequently, the weight starts to pile on (*see* Brian Wilson and Elvis). The more money they make, the more likely they are to suffer from 'coke bloat', where their weight balloons after gorging on sweets and junk food after week-long cocaine benders. Then their svelte frames disappear and they start to look like Demis Roussos in a funfair mirror.

A BLUFFER'S SURVIVAL GUIDE

Bluffing your way through a conversation about rock at a party or on a website discussion board is one thing, but being able to convincingly do it 'in the wild' at a festival or in a record shop is another thing entirely.

This is where your bluff mettle will be seriously tested, so you need to carefully plot out a strategy for survival – or else have an escape route if things go wrong.

For those instances where it's fight rather than flight, here are tips to survive when you go where rock fans roam freely.

FESTIVALS

Types of festival
What type of festival you go to will say a lot about the type of fan you are, so choose very cautiously. The fail-

safe choice, of course, is Glastonbury (call it 'Glasto' for added authenticity) because it's so broad and you can sniffily say that you prefer to avoid the 'Pyramid' stage, and spend time in the 'hidden' performance areas like The Rabbit Hole and The Crows Nest where you can actually see something, before lamenting how the 'spirit' has been lost with the 'mainstream' crowd who swamp it every year. (Of course, you've never been before.) Reading and Leeds suggest you enjoy listening to huge-selling, alt-rock bands like Green Day and Foo Fighters while hurling urine-filled bottles around like the world's worst juggler. Bestival implies you like fancy dress (no one likes fancy dress except people in fancy dress). End of the Road/Green Man/Latitude scream that you only like music made by desperately serious men in beards. Download is for metal fans and V Festival is like Channel 4 on a Saturday afternoon brought to horrifying life. There are an increasing number of 'boutique' festivals but there is no need to go there, as no one who goes has heard of any of the people playing. You will have to pretend you have, and it's a tiring omni-bluff to do that.

What to bring with you
Festivals (unless you go to any of the ones in the main parks in London) tend to involve camping, so you need to bring a tent or, if the budget will allow, a Winnebago (but everyone will see you as a part-timer if you sleep in one of these wheeled bungalows). You will not, however, be able to sleep as the noise of drunken people falling over is carefully scheduled to run all through

the night. Toilet paper after day two is worth more per gram than the pick-me-ups the bands are helping themselves to backstage, so bring plenty of rolls (they can also double up as a pillow/airbed). Alcohol, to numb the pain of having to stand around for hours in the rain while nothing happens, is essential. It will also aid sleep. Finally, remortgage your house and bring wads of tenners; festivals tend to work as a dry run for when the global economy completely implodes and inflation runs riot to the point where a burger costs £18,000 and a round of beers runs into six figures.

How to dress

If it's a UK festival, you need wellington boots, waders, sou'westers and a Victorian diving suit. During one of the days, however, the sun will escape from the Mediterranean and burn everyone to within an inch of their lives, so bring factor 40, flip-flops and a hat with a brim like the rings of Saturn. You must also wear a T-shirt, ideally an official T-shirt of the festival you are at, but from 20 years ago (you can get them on eBay, but do boil wash them thoroughly first) to look like you are an old hand. Better still, a T-shirt (with suspicious holes burned into it) of a band that is not playing that festival and has never played that festival. Also, bring at least 50 changes of socks to avoid trench foot.

Who to see and what to say

The first rule of festivals is to be toweringly blasé about the main stage headliners. This is where you need to do some research and find out when they played a small venue near you before anyone knew who they were. Then you can loudly proclaim, 'Yeah, I'm not going to see Arctic Monkeys/Elbow/The Black Keys as they'll not be the same band I saw play King Tut's in Glasgow in 2005 when only five people showed up' before sneaking off to a different part of the crowd to see them for the first time.

Another useful ruse is to randomly walk into a small tent on the first day, watch the first band you see and then loudly declare that they 'stole the festival weekend'. Finally, watch any band on the main stage around 3pm and describe them as 'pretty good' but note how they 'didn't really work in daylight'. That should just about cover it.

Who to avoid
Pretty much every band until the last 15 minutes of their 'set' (note: always call their performance a 'set') is to be avoided like a double dose of the plague. The majority of their set list will be weighted towards new songs and album tracks, but the last 15 minutes will be a frantic race through their Biggest Hits and, as such, will not be too tedious as you don't have to sit through a plodding piece the bass player wrote.

What not to buy when you're there
Do not buy a T-shirt while 'on site' as that will immediately mark you out as an arriviste. Equally avoid any kind of novelty headwear (hunter caps, foam jester hats, those beanie hats with dreadlocks sewn into them) and any kind of poster/lighter/keyring that has

a cannabis leaf logo on it. The absolute worst thing to buy is a pair of those voluminous trousers-cum-pyjama-bottoms that students on a gap year in India buy. In short: buy nothing at a festival.

What to say afterwards

Coming home shell-shocked after not being able to sleep or wash for three days will make you unable to speak for a few days. When the last traces of horror ebb away and the bends subside, friends and family will ask how it went. Do not start weeping uncontrollably and say, 'It was awful! It's like swimming in a septic tank for a weekend while the worst radio station in the world plays!' Instead, talk in vague, yet positive terms, about how there was a real 'sense of community' among the fans (when in reality it was like *Lord of the Flies* with lukewarm beer) and that it really showed you 'the power of music'. Then cheerily say you are already planning to go back next year while making a very clear mental note never to be within 5,000 miles – or even leave the house where you have running water, a bed and an operational toilet.

Randomly walk into a small tent on the first day, watch the first band you see and then loudly declare that they 'stole the festival weekend'.

RECORD SHOPS

Types of record shop
In order to convincingly bluff it as a real rock fan, you have to take your life in your hands and shop at a real record shop. No iTunes or Amazon or browsing the top 20 in your supermarket for you. Not even HMV (if it still exists). You have to go to an independent record shop hidden down a side street and smelling of broken dreams and patchouli oil. Such shops are something of a dying breed so you will have to do your research first and find your local one. By avoiding the internet and the high street you are 'making a statement' as a consumer, and just being seen in one of these shops will give you instant rock credibility. But once inside, it's far from a picnic. Strolling in is the easy part. …

The layout of the shop
A record shop is a topographically bewildering experience – but any nervousness and hesitancy on your part will immediately mark you out as a clueless interloper. So walk in a straight line to the first rack you see and make it look like this was where you had always planned to go. Lighting is intentionally low so be wary of tripping on steps or boxes of unpacked LPs; seasoned bluffers will know the store layout like the back of their hand. Do not walk up to the counter immediately and say, 'Do you have any music I might have heard of?'

How to skim through the racks

As with so many things in life, it's all in the wrist. The racks of vinyl in a record shop are whizzed through by regulars like a Vegas card sharp playing with a giant deck. Each section will be divided not just alphabetically but also by genre and sometimes by record label. This is a cunning layout plan to trick bluffers, so to be forewarned here is to be forearmed. Even if you have no idea what you're looking for, pick a section and flick through the albums using both hands and around every 15th one, pick it up, flip it over and study the tracks listed on the back while murmuring knowingly before putting it back. Do not go through the racks in order. Simply choose three or four in a non-sequential manner and repeat the skim-pause-look-at-15th-LP loop. Congratulations, you're browsing like a pro.

The counter staff

None shall pass. Counter staff at record shops are among the scariest people in the world. They can sniff out bluffers at 100 yards and, as such, are your natural enemies. They control the music system and always – always – look with pity and disdain at what you buy unless you go every day and spend hundreds of pounds a month there. They yearn to be either in rock bands or to run record labels, but life has conspired to trap them behind a counter all day with their equally frustrated colleagues. Never, ever attempt to make small talk with them. They only talk in catalogue numbers and rare Portuguese re-pressings of albums that only they will like or buy.

The other shoppers

Be careful. You might think these people are your brothers in arms. They are not. Instead they are locked into a Byzantine game of esoteric rock knowledge one-upmanship with each other. As they furiously flick through the racks they will simultaneously be flicking through the racks of their mind in a 'Got, got, got, need, got' fashion and they will never be complete until they have heard every record ever made and have an opinion on it. Do not strike up a conversation with them as they will see through you instantly. And then they will try to inculcate you with their obsessive beliefs.

How to ask for something and/or buy something

You should visit a store at least six times merely to browse before building up to buying anything. Like an athlete, you have to get warmed up and you don't run a marathon in slippers. Surreptitiously use the Shazam app on your phone to identify the music they are playing and mention it in passing just as you are leaving (say 'Oh, that [INSERT BAND NAME HERE] you were playing is so good. Love their stuff'). Be wary of buying white label releases (promotional discs or small niche releases which don't even have the track name on the label in the middle of the vinyl) as they are the bear traps in record shops and you'll have no idea what you're buying – a dead giveaway. Finally, record in bag, march purposefully out of the shop and never play it. It will almost certainly be terrible.

There's no point in pretending that you know everything about rock music – nobody does – but if you've got this far and absorbed at least a modicum of the information and advice contained within these pages, then you will almost certainly know more than 99% of the rest of the human race about what rock is, who plays it, where its roots lie, why it is a magnet for charlatans and imposters, and why it is a religion for millions of people throughout the world.

What you now do with this information is up to you, but here's a suggestion: be confident about your new-found knowledge, see how far it takes you, but above all have fun using it. You are now a bona fide expert in the art of bluffing about a musical genre which has more than its fair share of bluffers – both behind and in front of the microphone.

GLOSSARY

AAA An 'access all areas' pass means you can freely waltz into any room in the venue. Bearers never see the band as they are too busy trying to impress other people with AAA passes.

A-list Not a list, but the list a radio station compiles of the songs it will play the most in a given week. Pluggers' (*see* page 126) whole lives depend on getting a track on the A-list, not realising that, because the song is hammered to death for six weeks before release, everyone is utterly sick of it when it finally comes out.

A&R Stands for 'artists and repertoire'. These are the people at record companies who find, sign and develop 'talent'. Chronic inability to make any kind of decision means they are known as 'umm and errs'.

Advance What a label gives a band when they sign away their souls so they can eat. It is quickly frittered away on limos, champagne, parties, clothes and ludicrous lifestyle accessories. Profligate spending of this means bands rarely recoup (*see* 'Recoupment', page 126).

Agent Every band needs one and yet none of them are exactly sure what the agent actually does.

Airplay Not the high jinks and debauchery a band gets up to in an aeroplane, but what is played on radio.

Autotune A piece of recording software that 'corrects' vocal performances and slides them into the correct key if the singer is sounding like a swarm of wasps being chased by a pack of dogs around a cave.

Back catalogue Any record older than 18 months, where it will be subjected to shameless discounting, reissues, repackaging, anniversary editions, etc. to squeeze the last pips of cash out of it.

Backstage Seen by outsiders as the most exciting place imaginable, awash with rock stars and supermodels. In reality it's endless corridors full of bored people and a room where all you can do is eat lukewarm dips while sitting on a burst sofa.

Band call Another name for the soundcheck (*see* 'Soundcheck', page 128).

Bend A technique overused by guitarists, bending a string to stretch and warp a note. Features heavily in guitar solos.

Board (mixing board) An enormous Tardis-like desk that sits in studios and live venues where all the audio is fed through and mixed into an acoustic mortar attack.

Bono Talk Diminutive do-gooder Bono from U2 reportedly pinpoints acts on the cusp of success and then gives them a lecture on what to expect from fame and how to handle it. Currently helping the Pope.

Breaking (for a new act) Not splitting up or suffering a breakdown, this is when everything aligns and a band finally writes a song or an album that lots of people want to buy. Fewer than 10% actually make it.

Cans Archaic studio terminology for headphones, also used by fans who want to seem au fait with studio jargon.

Capo That little clippable collar guitarists put on their fretboard. In theory it heightens the pitch of strings but is frequently used by guitarists who only know a few chords but want to sound as if they know a lot more.

Click track A glorified metronome which (primarily) drummers can use in the studio or live to cover up the fact that they can't keep a steady beat.

Decks Fool yourself into thinking you are some hotshot radio or club DJ by calling record players 'decks'.

Door split Part of the labyrinthine way live music economics works in small venues; bands can either set a fee or take a split of money paid at the door after the venue 'covers its costs'. The band usually walks away with 75p in loose change and a button.

Dropped When the record label gets fed up with throwing money at bands and cuts off the supply. It's akin to being disinherited by a disappointed parent.

Encore Where live performance strays shamelessly into pantomime territory. The band walk off but they haven't played their hit single! Disaster! So the crowd cheers and the band comes out and plays it. Gig saved!

EPK Stands for electronic press kit. Pre-recorded generic interviews responding to bland questioning and given to radio and TV so they can edit around it and pretend they got an 'exclusive interview'.

Feedback Not adverse comments on a performance or record, but that ear-piercing noise that happens when an electric guitar is put too close to an amp and bad interference bends through the air.

Festival Taking place every weekend for the entire summer, they are pop-up cities of overpriced awfulness where all the year's rain falls and you only see 2% of the bands you paid to see.

Fruit and flowers A euphemism for 'recreational stimulants' and other nefarious expenditures. Thus called so they can be put through as expenses without the accountant having to call the police.

Gatefold The ideal format for a vinyl release, as the cardboard opens up like a gate and there is enormously pretentious artwork contained within to stare at while playing the record and powering through an 'infused cigarette'.

Gig A concert. Only your grandmother calls them 'concerts'. Everyone else has to call them 'gigs'.

Groupie Someone who provides 'executive relief' for touring musicians who immediately presume any woman within 50 miles wants to sleep with them.

Headline Not a story in a newspaper but what every band wants to be – the last act on the stage on a tour or at a festival.

Heritage acts A polite way to describe bands riddled with paunches and pattern baldness/hairy ears which are doing one last run around the venues to top up their pensions.

Indies Short for 'independent record label'. Music released on indies is somehow more 'real' and 'honest' that anything on a major.

LD The lighting director has the unenviable job of trying to make lumpen charisma-bypass musicians appear exciting on stage by using lights as surrogate exhilaration.

Lick Defined as 'a stock pattern or phrase' based typically around single notes rather than chords, thus marking them out as different from riffs (*see* 'Riff', page 127).

Majors Name for the biggest record labels in the world (Universal, Sony, Warner and EMI). Seen in dismissive terms as 'corporate' and 'mainstream'.

Manager The non-musician boss in charge of the band and their finances. He or she deals with labels, venues, promoters, etc. on the band's behalf and pockets 20% of their earnings as a result. Has a lot of babysitting to do.

Master The final recording of a song. Used to be held on giant rolls of tape and used to press the records; now they sit on a USB drive the size of a match.

Mechanicals Nothing to do with equipment but the name for royalties that songwriters get when recordings of their compositions are sold (or streamed); relating to the 'mechanical reproduction' of music.

Merch stall The stand at a gig where T-shirts, hoodies, posters, key rings and any number of tatty items designed to wring even more money out of fans are sold.

Middle eight The real sign of a songwriter is the ability to write a catchy middle eight. They tend to be eight bars long and are there to break up the verse/chorus repetition and give the song extra fizz. The 'I don't know why she's riding so high ...' bit in The Beatles' 'Ticket To Ride' is a classic example.

Midweeks The industry-circulated charts that show where a single or album is in the charts in the middle of the week (obviously). Whole careers can live or die on a mid-week position.

Mixer Responsible for how a recorded song sounds by

putting certain elements like vocals and guitars 'high' in the mix and lowering other parts like bass and keyboards to get a rounded sound. All musicians will claim their parts are always too 'low' in the mix. Always.

Monitors Those shell-like things on a stage facing the band which lets them hear what they are all playing so that, in theory, they are all playing the same song and roughly at the same time and speed.

Moshing Also known as 'slamdancing', this is a style of dance where audience members slam into each other. It usually happens in a 'mosh pit' in front of the stage and is associated with hardcore punk and heavy metal.

Option Refers to a record contract. Acts are generally signed for one or two albums but with 'options' for more albums. This means the label is under no obligation to pay for subsequent albums and can drop the band if they've not hit the sales expected of them.

PDs Short for 'per diems', the pocket money doled out to band members and crew on the road or in the studio each day and which they use to buy important things like cigarettes. And sweets.

Pickup No, not that sort, but a component on an electrical guitar that sends sound to speakers wirelessly without the need for lengthy cables that everyone trips over/gets wrapped up in like an electric mummy.

Platter Easy to confuse with backstage catering, this actually means a vinyl record (*see* 'Decks', page 122), and also means embarrassing superannuated radio DJs can talk about playing 'the platters that matter'.

Playlist List of songs radio stations play. If your song is not on there, a life of anonymity is yours for the taking.

Now overtaken by playlists on services like Spotify where, if you're not on any of the main ones, you might as well be dead.

Plugger Promotions person tasked with getting records played on radio or TV. Back when record companies had money, they spent a lot of time coming up with stunts and pranks to get a terrible record talked about and played. Giving money to DJs was traditionally the most reliable means.

Power chord The building block of much of rock music. Involves playing just two (possibly three) strings on a guitar (making that 'chug-chug-chug' sound) and so means any fool can play them – and often does.

Power trio A three-piece rock band with the singer playing guitar (or bass) and getting rid of the need for a second guitarist. Examples include The Jimi Hendrix Experience, The Jam, Motörhead, Nirvana and The Police.

Promo Short for 'promotion'. Covers press, radio and TV interviews as well as performances. Often involves sitting in hotel rooms answering the same questions over and over again for 40 different journalists.

Recoupment It's when a band has paid back its advance from its record label and can start to see royalties at long last (a rare occurrence, thanks to creative accounting).

Repertoire A fancy name for 'songs'.

Returns Unsold stock that even after desperate discounting, record shops just cannot shift. Less of an issue with downloads.

Rider All the grub, beer and changes of socks backstage a touring band can ever want. If it's not supplied by the venue, they are under no obligation to play the show. Famously, Van Halen insisted on bowls of M&Ms with all the brown ones removed.

Riff Defined as a short and repeated musical phrase and is the guitar part people try and 'sing' along with. The most famous is Deep Purple's 'Smoke On The Water'. All together now: 'Der-ner-ner ner-ner-ner-NER …'.

Riser The little stage on top of the stage where the drum kit goes, mainly because the drummer is miffed no one can see them stuck at the back.

Roadie The dogsbodies of the touring band. Dressed entirely in denim and band T-shirts, they get everything in and out of the venue and make sure everything works. Must always carry, under Roadie Law, a torch. And have a beard.

Royalties A percentage payment for record sales given to songwriters and recording artists. Like electricity, it's something artists know is there but they can't actually see.

Session Name given to a recording. Much like a concert must always be called a 'gig', any recording activity must be called a 'session'.

Set list List of songs a band will play live in order, written down IN BIG LETTERS and stuck on the floor of the stage by each musician, thereby increasing the chances of them all performing the same song at roughly the same time.

Shitters What touring musicians call money, partly a hangover of the pre-euro days where a trip round Europe would involve multiple currencies. Rather than remember the difference between francs, lira and drachmas, all money was called 'shitters' (as in 'Look – it's only three shitters for a packet of ciggies here').

Silver/gold/platinum Framed ornamental records given out for various sales of an album. In the UK, silver is for 60,000, gold for 100,000 and platinum for 300,000. 'Humble' musicians hang them in the toilet (in a direct eyeline with the coke tray).

SM Short name for a stage manager who is in charge of all technical aspects for a live show. Not to be confused with S&M which can also be found backstage.

Solo Where the guitarist (mainly) gets to do an over-indulgent display of how many notes he or she can play in as short a period of time as possible. Has mutated as other jealous band members insist on a drum solo or the very worst thing in music – a bass solo.

Soundcheck Where touring bands rush through a couple of songs before a show to make sure the equipment is working and the sound is being mixed properly from the room. Involves people listlessly saying 'One-two' into mics over and over again, peppered occasionally by a disinterested thump of a drum.

Spot Short for spotlight. What every band member wants trained on them every second they are on stage.

Stack Name for the pile of amps on the stage. The bigger the stack, the better the gig, or so runs the logic. Several bands are rumoured to have dummy amps there to make the stack seem bigger.

Toilet circuit Scatological name given to the series of small venues that bands have to drag themselves around time and time again in the hope of building a following.